TALES FROM THE
PHILADELPHIA EAGLES
SIDELINE

D1197884

TALES FROM THE
PHILADELPHIA EAGLES
SIDELINE

A COLLECTION OF THE GREATEST
EAGLES STORIES EVER TOLD

GORDON FORBES

SPORTS
PUBLISHING

Copyright © 2002, 2006, 2011 by Gordon Forbes

All Rights Reserved. No part of this book may be reproduced in any manner without the express written consent of the publisher, except in the case of brief excerpts in critical reviews or articles. All inquiries should be addressed to Sports Publishing, 307 West 36th Street, 11th Floor, New York, NY 10018.

Sports Publishing books may be purchased in bulk at special discounts for sales promotion, corporate gifts, fund-raising, or educational purposes. Special editions can also be created to specifications. For details, contact the Special Sales Department, Sports Publishing, 307 West 36th Street, 11th Floor, New York, NY 10018 or info@skyhorsepublishing.com.

Sports Publishing® is a registered trademark of Skyhorse Publishing, Inc.®, a Delaware corporation.

www.sportspubbooks.com

10 9 8 7 6 5 4 3

Library of Congress Cataloging-in-Publication Data is available on file.

ISBN: 978-1-61321-028-4

Printed in the United States of America

To June, my courageous wife, who fought leukemia for 13 ½ years without complaint; to Marie, my very special partner in the challenging years that have followed; and to my sons, Jim and Chris, who are chasing their own kind of Super Bowls in song and security.

CONTENTS

INTRODUCTION ix

Chapter 1
THE LEGENDS 1

Chapter 2
THE SUPERSTARS 21

Chapter 3
THE PLAYERS 63

Chapter 4
THE COACHES 117

Chapter 5
THE OWNERS 145

Chapter 6
OTHERS WHO SERVED 159

Chapter 7
**VICK'S BAG OF TRICKS HAS EAGLES
FEELING SUPER (AGAIN)** 173

Chapter 8
**25 THINGS YOU PROBABLY DIDN'T
KNOW ABOUT THE EAGLES** 181

ACKNOWLEDGMENTS 185

INTRODUCTION

They were the undisputed kings of the NFC East. In dominating style, the Philadelphia Eagles captured four straight division titles to launch the new millennium and seemed poised to win their first league title since 1960, the Chuck Bednarik-Norm Van Brocklin championship year.

Suddenly, they were in the Super Bowl, driven there by quarterback Donovan McNabb's golden season. But then it all fell apart. The Eagles lost Super Bowl XXXIX to Tom Brady and the New England Patriots, losing four turnovers in a scattershot performance. Their anticipated celebration up Broad Street became an off-season of bickering and finger-pointing. Terrell Owens, their opinionated receiver, reversed roles. He began throwing nasty insults. By Owens' choice, McNabb caught most of them.

Stunningly, the Eagles plunged to the bottom of the division in 2005, Coach Andy Reid's first losing season since 1999, his rookie year. Owens, better known as T.O., was suspended, missed the final nine games, and was then cut after a tumultuous 6-10 season. McNabb struggled with a sports hernia. Kicker David Akers pulled a hamstring. Half-back Brian Westbrook sprained a foot. Receiver Todd Pinkston tore an Achilles tendon.

But now, in Reid's eighth year, all the injuries, as well as the Eagles' damaged psyche, seem to have healed. There are new faces all around. Reid always had speed. And he has McNabb, who has thrown 134 touchdown passes in seven years. "I'm not here to win friends," McNabb said, ever the persuasive team leader. "I'm here to win games."

Reid denied that this could be a divided team after T.O.'s departure. "There are no hangovers from last year," proclaimed Reid. So, as the Eagles headed for another of Reid's fast-paced training camps, there was guarded optimism through the ranks. Living up to a long tradition of tough, relentless play, the Eagles will try to dominate the way they used to dominate.

Foremost, the Eagles must fly to the ball and hit on defense. They must hustle to the whistle. They must return to the days of Bednarik and the late

Reggie White and a wild and wonderful special teams banger named Vince Papale. In those years, the last play of every game was like the first play of a Super Bowl. Those now-suffering Eagle fans, the screamers from the sprawling Northeast and the deep thinkers from the Main Line, will demand it.

Yet if there is a lack of effort, Philadelphians can become raucous boo-birds and bolt with the quickness of Steve Van Buren, the great running back on those Eagle championship teams of the late '40s. They will jeer and unleash strange objects, as they did in the late '60s when Joe Kuharich was coaching and losing and sputtering original lines like, "You win some, you lose some, and some you teeter-totter."

Kuharich's reference to a teeter-totter only provoked the fans. Their city is tough and decisive and relentless in its drive to escape its fun-poking past. Its invented cult hero is Rocky, the movie boxer. The passionate Eagles fan prefers a powerful five-yard run or a smashing good tackle to a 15-yard reverse or a tricky flea-flicker. Its living legends are Chuck Bednarik and Steve Van Buren. Fittingly, both were two-way players.

Bednarik, known as Concrete Charley, was a great linebacker and center, doubling on defense out of necessity. Van Buren, the Walter Payton of his era except on payday, was a great running back and safety. Everybody filled 60-minute roles in the pre-television '40s, when penny-pinching teams played with 35-man rosters.

The fans, even those too young to have been in the house, cling to two memorable plays. Who can forget the sight of Bednarik perched atop Green Bay's Jim Taylor as time ran out in the 1960 championship game? Or of Van Buren slashing through the snowflakes for the only touchdown at old Shibe Park in the 1948 title game against the Chicago Cardinals? The young Eagles fans remember because the plays are handed down generation to generation, like fine jewelry.

I never saw Bednarik or Van Buren play. But I've seen some films and heard some tales that almost ring with their power and will. Oh, I've felt Bednarik's famous elbow during some pickup basketball games at the University of Pennsylvania, his alma mater. I can only imagine how it felt to take the full body.

I covered the Eagles for the *Philadelphia Inquirer* from 1966-81, a 16-year period of changing coaches and changing quarterbacks. Only three of the 12 first-round draft picks from that mostly dismal era became Pro Bowlers. Then a little whip of a guy named Dick Vermeil arrived in 1976 with a persuasive way and a plan. Vermeil coached the Eagles to the level of respectability, then took them to their first Super Bowl in 1980. But on that forgettable day of January 25, 1981, the Eagles looked like stiff second graders posing for a class photo when they were introduced. They were indeed tense and were dominated by the Oakland Raiders, 27-10, in Super Bowl XV.

So the Eagles have gone 45 years without an NFL championship. Led by Van Buren, quarterback Tommy Thompson, who was legally blind in one eye, and a smothering defense that produced eight shutouts, the Eagles won it all in 1948 and 1949. Their only other title came in 1960. With Bednarik playing both ways, they edged the Green Bay Packers, 17-13, to hand Vince Lombardi his only playoff defeat.

Over the 16 years that I worked the beat, the Eagles averaged six wins per year. They were dreadful on the road, with a 40-74-4 record. Yet rarely did I sense that an Eagles team ever quit. One of the few times was a 62-10 road loss to the New York Giants in 1972. The night before, coach Ed Khayat invited me to share a beer at a cozy bar near Central Park. A patron recognized Khayat and introduced himself. "Do you think we've got a chance tomorrow?" Khayat asked. "Sure, Coach," the customer nodded. "Good," Khayat smiled. "That makes two of us."

Over the years, the Eagles played some other clunkers like that. The most humiliating was a 1975 Monday nighter against the Los Angeles Rams, the western division champions. The water-cooler issue all week was whether the Eagles had been dogging it, a claim that coach Mike McCormack did not totally reject. Accordingly, some fans brought inflated dog bones to the game and batted them around the stands like balloons. Others tossed real dog biscuits on the field. Still others waved "Alpo" signs for the television cameras. The Rams had the Eagles on a leash all night in a 42-3 romp. Dogs, indeed.

Yet there has almost always been a tenacity about the Eagles, even in their down years. The fans came to appreciate overachieving players like Tom Woodeshick, a reckless fullback from West Virginia, who used to punch out parking meters with his fists in college, and Ike Kelley, a stumpy special teams banger from Ohio State, who delighted in dumping Cleveland kicking legend Lou Groza on kickoffs.

After their Super Bowl loss and four coaching changes, the Eagles discovered a coaching gem in Andy Reid. The team that Reid now coaches is a throwback to an earlier era. In Philadelphia, they don't judge the Eagles by speed or by size, but by toughness. One jarring hit and you're a hero from Manayunk to the Main Line.

THE LEGENDS

CHUCK BEDNARIK

It has been 44 years since he stripped off his pads and his famous No. 60 game jersey. Yet the saga of Chuck Bednarik endures, indeed, even grows, as the man known as Concrete Charley contemplates life long after football. Bednarik still embraces the game that made him famous from the celebrity edge, attending trade shows and charity banquets and hawking his autobiography.

At those highly popular autograph shows, he sells a famous eight-by-ten photograph. It shows Frank Gifford, stretched motionless on the cold Yankee Stadium turf after being knocked out by Bednarik's smashing tackle in a November 20, 1960 game against the New York Giants.

About 14 years ago, Gifford was roasted at the annual Valerie Fund dinner, a charity affair named after Valerie Goldstein, a little girl from Warren, New Jersey, who died of cancer. Bednarik was invited to the roast. "I came up with a great idea," Bednarik recalled. "I told the people there that when I was introduced, they should turn the lights off for five or ten seconds." Confusion momentarily gripped the audience. But when the lights came back on, it was Bednarik's cue. "Frank," he said, pausing for just the right effect, "does that ring a bell?" Gifford grinned sheepishly. But his wife,

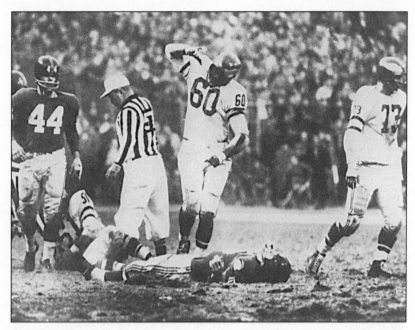

Chuck Bednarik (60) celebrates his famous tackle of Frank Gifford on November 20, 1960, while Ed Khayat (73) walks off, and Chuck Weber (51) grabs the ball.

Kathie Lee, "didn't get it," according to Dave Klein, the longtime football writer who founded the Valerie Fund.

Bednarik and Gifford occasionally meet, the last time during a 2000 celebration at the Pro Football Hall of Fame in Canton, Ohio. "I walked up to him, and he looked at me and said, 'I made you famous, didn't I?'" Bednarik, however, says the play became legendary only because of the circumstances. "I did it in New York," he said. "That's where all the notoriety comes from. And I did it to the top honcho. He just happened to be there and the pass was thrown to him. I waffled him cleanly. It could have been Kyle Rote. It could have been anybody. That's a dangerous pass, that down-and-in. You start looking at the ball coming from the quarterback and here comes somebody from the opposite side. You can get killed on those."

"He just cold-cocked Frank," said linebacker Bob Pellegrini, whose injury sent Bednarik into the game to play defense. "The ball flew one way and

[Gifford] flew the other. It was the best hit I ever saw. [Bednarik] was jumping up and down because of the fumble."

Bednarik's big hit forced the turnover that clinched the game for the Eagles. Afterwards, Bednarik received the scare of his life. Instinctively, he headed for the Giants dressing room to check on Gifford. "Somebody in the stands had a heart attack," Bednarik said. "I wanted to go over and see how Frank was doing. Somebody came out and said, 'He's dead.' I said to myself, 'Holy crap.' I remember going into shock. Of course, then I saw Frank. He didn't seem to mind too much. I was just sorry it happened. Believe me, it wasn't intentional. And I didn't jump up and down like [Mark] Gastineau did."

What irked some New Yorkers, players and fans alike, was the sight of Bednarik punching his fist through the air. Bednarik can explain his celebration. "I saw Chuck Weber, our linebacker, fall on the ball. My back was turned [to Gifford]. When I saw Weber with the ball, I turned around, clenched my fist and yelled, 'This [bleeping] game is over.' I could have gloated over him but I didn't. I never saw him unconscious."

Bednarik has sold an estimated 3,400 photos of the hit on Gifford. He charges $10 for the highlight shot and says requests keep coming in. But Bednarik has no similar photo of the other less-than-classic tackle he made on Green Bay's Jim Taylor in the 1960 championship game. "Pictures," he said, "it's ridiculous. Joe Montana and all the top quarterbacks charge $50 for a photo. If I charged $25 for mine, I wouldn't get any money."

Only seconds were left in the Packers game. The Eagles led, 17-13, on Ted Dean's five-yard run, but Bart Starr drove the Packers to the Eagle 22-yard line under enormous pressure. "Starr went back to throw," said Bednarik. "There were only like 20 seconds left. Everybody was covered by our defensive backs. When Jimmy Taylor swung out of the backfield, I took off. A couple of our defensive backs came up and tried to knock him down. I came up and wrapped myself around him. I could see the clock above the east stands. It went six...five...four...three...two...one. He was trying to get up. When it hit zero, I said to Taylor, 'You can get up now. This [bleeping] game is over.'"

It was the same line that Bednarik had uttered after the Gifford hit. Indeed, the plays that Chuck Bednarik executed still rank as the two most famous tackles in Eagle history. Bednarik's game against the Packers ranks perhaps as the most memorable of them all since he went both ways—58 minutes as an offensive center and defensive middle linebacker.

"I was in awe of Chuck," says former linebacker Maxie Baughan, reflecting on his rookie season. "We would come on the field and Chuck would be waiting for us. He'd say, 'Let's go...let's get together.' If he was tired, he never let it show."

After all of these years, Bednarik is still considered the greatest of all Eagles, a distinction that he willingly embraces. But there is also an anger within the man. Bednarik hasn't seen an Eagles game since 1982, when Dick Vermeil left as head coach. "I could not care less," he said. "I've lost my desire to watch pro football. They are overpaid and underplayed. It's ridiculous. When I see these guys getting $20 million signing bonuses and five-year contracts, it drives me mad. I got a $3,000 bonus and a $10,000 salary, and I thought I was rich. They [bleep] me off. They do a little jitterbug dance after a tackle, and it drives me insane."

Bednarik has only sweet words to say about the current head coach, Andy Reid. Yet he refuses to visit Reid's fast-paced training camp even though he lives 15 minutes from Lehigh University, the club's training site. Bednarik remembers someone finding 1,500 copies of his autobiography in a warehouse. He thought it would be fitting if he signed 50 of the books and sold them to the Eagles to distribute to the players. The cut-rate price was $10.

"Chuck, I can't do that," owner Jeffrey Lurie said, according to Bednarik. "You can't give gifts to the players."

"What would it have cost him, $500?" asked Bednarik. "I'm through with him. And the hell with the game. I'm not going to watch those guys jitterbug like that. My favorite team is Lehigh University. My favorite sport is college wrestling. Lehigh was ranked sixth in the country. Lehigh is like the Ivies, all student athletes. The other schools, they get only 300-350 on the SATs and the coach doesn't give a damn. He just wants them to play football."

Bednarik keeps talking, keeps knocking the pro game and the major college game. "I never use the name of God in vain," he says. "I'm a devout Catholic. But I use the F-word; I use it constantly. It's just nasty."

He has fallen hard for Lehigh...except when the Eagles are conducting their summer training camp there. He remembers when Dick Vermeil arrived in 1976 and within 24 hours invited him and his wife to lunch. And then Vermeil invited Bednarik to be an honorary assistant coach, charting plays on the sideline at home and away games.

"He was a helluva coach," said Chuck Bednarik. "When Dick Vermeil left the Eagles, I left and I've never been back."

STEVE VAN BUREN

The game that Steve Van Buren remembers was all about toughness. The tougher team won. Not the fastest, or the biggest, or necessarily the smartest, but the team that inflicted the most punishment. That's the way Van Buren liked it. And that's the way the Eagles used him in their drive to two consecutive league championships in 1948-49.

"The last two years I played with 10-12 shots of Novocaine every game," Van Buren once told me in a revealing one-hour interview. "At one time I'd get it in my toe, ankle and ribs, all on the same side. I had four broken ribs and taped those. I had been operated on for a broken toe and they used to put tape and sponge under it. Then I broke those four ribs in my first game back. Then the ankle went. Other teams knew I was hurt. Sometimes I was groaning so much after a tackle that the other guys felt sorry for me. I played in pain in about half of the games in my career. You'd get used to the needles. The only time it bothered me was when the doc would hit the bone. They'd bend when they hit the bone."

Van Buren played in the pre-television era, when they called it rock 'em-sock 'em football. "He ran over a lot of guys and knocked them coo-coo," said Al Wistert, the tackle. "He was our ticket." The Eagles were one of the league's best teams, with four Hall of Fame players (Van Buren, center Alex Wojciechowicz, end Pete Pihos, rookie linebacker/center Chuck Bednarik) and a Hall of Fame coach, Earl "Greasy" Neale. Yet they were a bust at the gate, losing money every year. Van Buren's top salary was $15,000. He signed for that much in 1948 and never made a nickel more, even though he led the league in rushing for three straight years.

"I made under $100,000 for my entire career," he said. "The first year, I made $4,000, with no bonus. I wanted to play in Philly and money didn't matter." He was offered $15,000 to play in the rival All-America Conference after a spectacular Orange Bowl game. Instead, he joined the Eagles, in effect taking a 73-percent cut in pay to play in the NFL. And there was Van Buren's bizarre habit of refusing to sign checks that he got for endorsements. A hat company once offered him $300 to endorse its product. Van Buren declined. "Everyone knows I don't wear a hat," he explained.

More than 50 years after his last carry in 1951, Van Buren has few, if any, reminders of his glory days. "I've got a big picture of myself some kid made," he told me. "And another one given to me on Van Buren Day. A couple of trophies, too. Outside of these, I haven't got anything. I didn't believe in

Steve Van Buren, who never earned more than $15,000 per season, led the league in rushing four times, including a 1,146-yard season in 1949.

saving anything else. A lot of times, I didn't bother picking up the trophies. The old Eagles had one that I just never brought home."

So Steve Van Buren, now 80 and a devoted horse player, is left with his memories. And what memories! He led the league in rushing four times, including a 1,146-yard season in 1949. He scored 18 touchdowns in 1945 (still an Eagles record). He rushed for 205 yards against Pittsburgh in 1949, another club record, and rushed for 196 yards on a mud-clogged field against the Los Angeles Rams in the 1949 title game.

"You could feel when you had to lower your shoulder and run into them," said Van Buren. "The Bears had a player named Fred Davis. He weighed about 260 and wrestled in the off-season—a strong boy. I once hit him with a shoulder and knocked him out. Nobody really gave me too tough a time. They had a little linebacker in Pittsburgh; I think he was named Hogan. He was six feet, about 220 pounds, a squatty-shape guy. He caught me off balance one time and knocked the [bleep] out of me."

Van Buren gave a lot more than he took. He once told Larry Cabrelli and Al Wistert to forget about their double-team assignment in a game against the Steelers. He had a nasty plan to get even with one of the Steelers' tackles who had unnecessarily roughed him up. There had been, as quarterback Allie Sherman once told it, "a lot of knees and elbows after the play, as well as head-twisting and fists to the face." Van Buren took Sherman's handoff after a fullback fake and left his victim motionless on his back. "I got a look at him," said Sherman. "Both eyes were actually spinning around."

Of all Van Buren's runs, none is more famous than his five-yard burst through a snowstorm that beat the Chicago Cardinals, 7-0, in the 1948 title game. To this day, Van Buren seems amused that the run is perceived as one of his toughest touchdowns.

"I had hardly gotten to the line when the hole closed," he said. "So I ran inside. Everybody for years would tell me how I fought and clawed for the touchdown. Actually, I was hardly touched. The hole used to close a lot, not because Wistert and [Pete] Pihos didn't block, but because the other teams played the play."

Van Buren's feats seem more remarkable when you consider that he played safety on defense, often sapping his energy. It was also the era of the 12-game season, four games fewer than teams play today. Knee surgery was often delayed until after the season.

"The object of the game then, as it is now, is to beat the hell out of the opposing team," said Van Buren. He relished every chance he got to give them the shoulder, the forearm, the elbow and the high knee. The wonder is that it took 19 years for the Hall of Fame selectors to recognize his greatness with a football in his hands.

NORM VAN BROCKLIN

The perception remains that Norm Van Brocklin had no warm side. He ranted after defeats, of course. As a coach, he sometimes spilled his pregame coffee on the hands of some players, one of his motivational tricks. Van Brocklin, one of the game's great quarterbacks, coached at Minnesota and Atlanta. But Tommy McDonald, who caught so many of Van Brocklin's touchdown passes, says the trade with the Los Angeles Rams that brought Van Brocklin east was predicated on him coaching the Eagles when he retired.

"I was told that [NFL commissioner] Bert Bell got on the phone and told Van Brocklin that if he came and played three or four years, the Eagles would give him a shot at the coaching job." Bell, who owned the original Eagles (known as the Frankford Yellowjackets before 1933), died in 1959, the year before Van Brocklin led his old team to a world championship. In 1961, the year Van Brocklin was supposed to exchange his pads for a coaching whistle, the job went to Nick Skorich. Van Brocklin ended up coaching the expansion Vikings and enjoyed a win over Skorich's second Eagles team in 1962.

"I'd put him in the Triple-A category as one of the best quarterbacks who ever lived," said Chuck Bednarik, the Eagles' Hall of Fame center/linebacker. "Van Brocklin, Bobby Layne, Y. A. Tittle, Otto Graham, and Johnny Unitas, they're Triple-A."

Van Brocklin played only three seasons with the Eagles. But that 1960 team, with its sense of disdain for the other side and its rowdy personality, attained a mythical niche in Philadelphia sports history. Van Brocklin, of course, was its legendary leader. The Dutchman, as he was called, brought the Eagles from behind five times during their drive to the title. "I'd put him in the class with Unitas," said McDonald. "But Unitas had Alan Ameche and Lenny Moore to run. Everybody knew we were going to pass. But could they stop him? Oh, no. We knew we were never out of a game as long as we had Dutch. He always came up with the big play."

Eddie Khayat, a defensive tackle on the championship team, still raves about Dutch Van Brocklin. "One thing people fail to see," said Khayat, "is

Although he spent only three seasons in Philadelphia, Norm Van Brocklin is remembered as the legendary leader of the Eagles' 1960 NFL championship team.

that a quarterback has to be the toughest guy on the team. He doesn't need to be a fighter, like a Bednarik or J. D. Smith, with fisticuffs. But he has to be just tough. Dutch was so smart and so tough, and he brought out the best in everybody. He taught everybody how to win. He was a great leader, the first one to practice every day."

Pete Retzlaff, the tight end, confirmed that Van Brocklin was much more than just the team's passing arm. "He had authority," said Retzlaff. "When Buck Shaw gave us something new to use, he'd turn to Van Brocklin and say, 'That OK with you, Dutch?' When that happened, the message came through about who the authority was on the team."

Van Brocklin's career began when he and Bob Waterfield were the Rams' quarterbacks. Hollywood types loved to mingle with the famous Rams players in the Coliseum locker room after home games. Yet of all the 12 seasons he played, 10 of them Pro Bowl seasons, his best was the run to the title in 1960. He retired with a passing record of 23,611 yards and 173 touchdowns.

And that warm side of Van Brocklin? Before leaving Minnesota to coach in Atlanta, the Van Brocklins made plans to adopt three young, deprived children. Eventually, Shelly Joe, five, Allen, four, and Randy, 17 months, moved into Van Brocklin's 174-acre pecan farm in Social Circle, Georgia.

"People didn't know the inside of the man," said McDonald. "Van Brocklin wasn't the acid-tongued guy that people think he was."

Norm Van Brocklin died in 1983 of a massive heart attack, when he should have been in his prime as a coach. He was 57.

PETE PIHOS

When the Eagles needed a first down and the defense was jammed inside to stop Steve Van Buren, there was only one option left. Get the ball somewhere near Pete Pihos, who would dutifully haul it in to keep the drive going.

Those who watched Pihos in his prime years of 1953-54 saw one of pro football's great ends. You never left the stadium raving about Pihos' speed, but about his clever moves and hands. Yet, ask Pihos about his foot speed and he replies, "I was fast enough."

Pihos caught 63, 60, and 62 passes in his final three seasons, leading the league twice and tying for the lead in the middle year. "Back in '47, '48 and through to '52, it was offense and defense," he said. "All of us played two

After three consecutive 60-catch seasons, Pete Pihos took Joe DiMaggio's advice and retired at the age of 32 in 1955.

ways. On defense, I just kept up with it. It was not like it was as tough playing on the end. Back then, you only had 33 players."

Pihos was so good at his trade that he was a six-time Pro Bowler and earned All-Pro honors as a defensive end in 1952 when the Eagles needed him to stuff the run. In 1955, his final season, he caught 62 passes, the equivalent of an 82-catch year in a 16-game season. He now lives in Winston-Salem, North Carolina.

"Joe DiMaggio was close with me," he said. "Sometime in March in 1955, Dean Martin and Jerry Lewis were playing a show in Atlantic City. The owner invited me to attend. They had a great show. And guess who walked in? Joe DiMaggio. It was just super meeting him. He told me, 'Pete, quit when you're on top.' I said, 'I'm fine. I'll go when I feel like it.'"

Taking DiMaggio's advice, Pihos retired to Winston-Salem after that season. He was only 32. He had earned two world championships and shared so many memories of going into sports battles with padded warriors who loved to mix it up. "Most of them are now so far away from me," said Pihos. "We just try to keep ourselves going. I'm happy. I do what I want to do. My health, I'm fine. My knees are fine, too. I take two pills a day, one every morning and the other at night. They're good pills."

Pihos was asked why specifically he needed to take the pills. "I don't know," he said. "My wife knows all about that."

TOM BROOKSHIER

The place to be on Mondays was Donohue's, a loud bar located at 63rd and Chestnut Streets. "That was part of [Norm] Van Brocklin's season," said Tom Brookshier, the Eagles' adventurous cornerback who loved to pounce on a receiver's tendermost spots. "He had to take his kid to Friends School on Monday morning, even with a previous hangover. We went to every after-hours place on Sunday night, about 14 to 18 of us. The guys would get into fights every other day."

Half of the team lived at the Walnut Park Plaza, an apartment complex not far from Donohue's. "Dutch would call them up at eight o'clock in the morning. He'd tell them to meet at Donohue's bar at high noon," Brookshier said. "They'd tell Dutch, 'We'll be there if our wives can get us up.'"

Van Brocklin was always in charge of the social festivities and the pace of the afternoon. "He could be a devil," said Brookshier. "One time he called up [sportscaster] Bill Campbell and invited him down. Bill got all dressed up

After his career as an adventurous cornerback who loved to pounce on a receiver's most tender spots, Tom Brookshier found success in the broadcast booth.

and put on his toupee. Before he arrived, Van Brocklin put a bucket of beer above the transit. Campbell got soaked and lost his toupee." The rowdy Eagles laughed it up and raised their glasses one more time.

On another Monday of fun and games, sportswriter Jack McKinney, an accomplished boxer, squared off with Billy Ray Barnes, a tough running back. Cooler heads prevailed and the bar talk continued. It was all part of Van Brocklin's way of bringing the Eagles together. They were a close team, feeding off each other's needling and anger to win it all in 1960.

"I think we lost our first ball game and then won nine in a row," said Brookshier. "I think we came from behind every damn game. In Cleveland, the wind was coming off the lake that day. My roommate happened to be Bobby Walston, our kicker. He brought a pair of pliers and pulled off the injured big toenail on his kicking foot before the game. I didn't think he could kick at all. But Van Brocklin put together one last drive. I remember he threw the ball into our bench one time to stop the clock. [Coach] Buck Shaw figured we needed a touchdown with Walston's foot and said, 'We could have used that [down] one'."

Suddenly, Shaw waved Walston and holder Sonny Jurgensen onto the field. "It was a 38-yarder, with a gale wind blowing and a lousy frozen field," said Brookshier. "Walston limped out there. The snap was only fair, and Sonny [Jurgensen] had trouble getting to it. The kick barely cleared the bar, carried over by the crazy wind. We won it [31-29]. I remember thinking, the way we won that game, anything is possible, baby. Jimmy Brown had 250 yards or so that day. We felt if we could beat a team like that, maybe we could win the damn championship."

How tight were the Eagles? Brookshier recalled a preseason game played in Roanoke, Virginia. A group of players, including Clarence Peaks, boarded the hotel elevator. Peaks, a black running back, was told he needed to step out and use the freight elevator.

"Where's the freight elevator?" asked Billy Ray Barnes, a North Carolinian. "We'll all take the freight elevator." Those Eagles did, counting Peaks as a brother of their family.

Brookshier, who went on to a career as a television sportscaster, enjoyed the 25th anniversary reunion of the '60 team. But he was saddened by the absence of Don Burroughs, Bobby Freeman, and some other Eagles.

"They only allowed them three [plane] tickets," said Brookshier. "Most of the guys came back, but not all of them. I'd love to see us get together again.

But now some of them have trouble walking up and down the stairs." And, of course, Donohue's closed long ago.

REGGIE WHITE

Reggie White thought he had seen every imaginable blocking scheme until he lined up against the Washington Redskins in the late '80s. The Redskins' pet play, of course, was known as 60 Counter-Gap. It caused confusion for the defense because of the misdirection created by the line flow. The Redskins' center, right guard, right tackle, and tight end all slant-blocked to the left, creating a wall; the left guard and left tackle pulled to the right ahead of the runner, who started with a jab step the other way to momentarily freeze the defense.

"When we lined up in that 46 [defense], the Redskins would slant their line a lot," said White. "Remember their off-tackle [the counter-gap]? They'd pass protect doing that against me. The line would slide and make it difficult. You couldn't put a move on anybody."

White was the best defensive lineman in Eagles history, a 285-pound athletic type with quick feet and enormous upper-body strength. I once saw White chase and catch scrambler Doug Flutie clear across the field with his burst when they both played in the United States Football League. At the Pro Bowl one year (White was a Pro Bowler 13 times in his 15-year career), he jumped into the receiver's line and ran downfield for a deep pass. The ball floated down over the wrong shoulder, but White did a little pirouette and made a twisting catch in the end zone. Wide receivers 100 pounds lighter should be so agile.

His future ticket to the Hall of Fame, of course, was his pass rush. He still holds the league career sack record of 198 set over a 15-year career. "Let's see, I used the bull [rush], the swim, the double-slap on the nose [tackle], slapping one shoulder then coming back and slapping the other, the slap-and-rip, and the club," said White. "I used just about every move except the head slap." Which was, of course, illegal. But what Reggie White did to opposing tackles, guards, and tight ends legally must have seemed illegal. "I figured if I could connect on two moves," said White, "if I could physically do that, I could dominate a guy."

He played on a great defense with the Eagles, coached by Buddy Ryan and brought together by a unique love for each other. The rush line featured White and Clyde Simmons outside and Jerome Brown and Mike Pitts inside.

Reggie White, who retired as the NFL's all-time leader in sacks, played on a great Eagles defense in the early '90s before moving on to the Green Bay Packers.

In 1991, the year after Ryan was dismissed, White had 15 sacks, and the defense totaled 55. The unit, which sent White, Brown, and Simmons, as well as corner Eric Allen and linebacker Seth Joyner, to the Pro Bowl, led the league in rushing defense (71.0 yards per game) and passing defense (150.8 yards per game). Yet the Eagles missed the playoffs in the year of the fallen quarterback. Randall Cunningham went down in the first game with torn knee ligaments. Jim McMahon followed in the fifth game with the same injury. The Eagles went to Brad Goebel, a rookie, then back to McMahon and finally to Jeff Kemp for two starts when McMahon broke several ribs.

"It was a very difficult year," said White. "We had so much talent that we could have won the big game. We won 10 games, and I think [the defense] literally won all 10 of those games. If we had Randall in there, or even Jimmy Mac, we could have won the whole thing."

There were training camp holdouts. Buddy Ryan, the defensive guru, was gone. They scored only 26 points in a four-game losing streak with Goebel and gimpy-kneed Jim McMahon at quarterback. So Reggie White sat down and began thinking about his future and about that Super Bowl ring that he desperately wanted. Two years later, he jumped to Green Bay and got it.

"It's something that had to be done," said White, who engaged owner Norman Braman in a bitter contract dispute before leaving. "I remember Angelo Cataldi and Tony Bruno, you know, the guys on WIP radio, put together a rally for me. There were 5,000 people there. They wanted to see me come back. I loved the fans a lot. I don't know if the Philadelphia fans know how much I loved them. I remember Norman [Braman] calling me at my home in Tennessee and saying he was willing to negotiate. Two weeks later, he said, 'I'm not embarking on that soap opera.' A lot of fans think I left just to leave. I just wish I had [Jeffrey] Lurie there. I think he would have done everything to keep me."

White promised that if he won a Super Bowl with Green Bay, he would enter the Hall of Fame as a Packer. "I would love to go in as an Eagle," he said. "But I made this promise. I hope Green Bay honors me the way I deserve to be honored. The one negative is that they seem to wait until the players are dead."

White's words were tragically prophetic. On December 26, 2004, Reggie White died at his home in Cornelius, North Carolina of a respiratory ailment that had affected his sleep for several years. The great pass-rusher and spiritual leader was 43.

"He was the best defensive lineman who ever played the game," said Buddy Ryan, White's former Eagles coach. Reid, who was in Green Bay when White arrived, agreed. "He changed games," said Reid. "He may have been the best player I've ever seen," said Brett Favre, the Packers' legendary quarterback.

When White signed with the Packers, general manager Ron Wolf remembered taking him to a local Red Lobster for a seafood dinner. "There were no limousines," said Wolf. "He was shown Green Bay as Green Bay was. He appreciated that. He saw that he was dealing with genuine people."

White was ordained as a minister at age 17. Naturally, they started calling him the Minister of Defense for all of those sacks and tackles. He was still deeply involved with religion and a squeaky-clean life style but had begun a re-evaluation stage at the time of his death. "There are some things that I don't like," he said. "Not that I've stopped seeing God. But I'm staying home more and reading a lot. I understand things more."

In his last endeavor, White had become the chairman of a long-distance phone company headquartered in Oklahoma City, "We have 25,000 subscribers," he had told me. "Fifteen percent of the profits go back to the ministries."

White was elected to the Pro Football Hall of Fame on February 4, 2006. The vote was unanimous, 39 ayes.

ALEX WOJCIECHOWICZ

The career of Alex Wojciechowicz is steeped in Eagles lore. And with each passing year, his name takes on a mythological place in pro football history, as if he were Thor, the Scandinavian god of thunder. Maybe it's his name, often twisted by announcers. Or maybe that he anchored   Fordham's legendary "Seven Blocks of Granite," a line that included Vince Lombardi. Or maybe his style, rough and punishing. Or that he once played in four games within a week. Whatever the reason, Wojie, as he was called, has come to be synonymous with great center and linebacking play.

Wojie played in an era of two-way iron men, when players were nicknamed "Ox," "Bucko," "Pickles," "Bullet," and "Hunk." He was a first-round pick of the Detroit Lions in 1938, but his biggest years were with the Eagles, who won two world championships using Wojie strictly as a linebacker. "He was the toughest guy on the team," once said fullback Jack

Hinkle. "He looked like a big, shaggy dog. A sad-eyed St. Bernard. But he'd rip your head off."

Jim Crowley, one of Notre Dame's famous Four Horsemen, advised Wojciechowicz not to shorten his name. "Keep it as it is," said Crowley, then Fordham's head coach. "You'll always be remembered." Crowley was right. The tongue-twisting name remains somewhat mystical. At one time, he thought about shortening it to "Wojack." But he took Crowley's advice.

"I get a thrill out of playing defense," said Wojie, a six-footer with exceptional speed. "Like all the others, I get a kick out of body contact." Later, before his death in 1992, he agonized over his inability to play golf in his retirement years. "I'd rather have played golf and become a pro," he said. "But because of my football injuries, I can't even play golf anymore."

After leaving pro football, Wojie helped to organize the NFL Alumni Association, a group that created the dire need fund for ex-players down on their luck. He also worked to gain pension benefits for old-timers. Wojciechowicz was elected to the Hall of Fame in 1968, three years before his old college teammate, Vince Lombardi. Actually, Wojie never thought much of Lombardi's skills and grew to resent the accolades received by his old Fordham linemate.

In a letter to Curt Gowdy, the announcer, Wojie wrote: "Vince deserves all the credit in the world, but he was really only a pretty good college football player. I can't believe that anybody truly thought that Lombardi was the significant member of the legendary 'Seven Blocks of Granite.'"

The letter was written without bitterness. Indeed, Wojie personally had the grass replaced twice on Lombardi's grave and was active in raising funds to build a gymnasium in his honor.

2

THE SUPERSTARS

BUCKO KILROY

"In the '40s and '50s, it was smash-mouth, or mash-mouth, football," explained Francis Joseph "Bucko" Kilroy, the NFL's smash-mouther of them all from 1943-55. "The rules were different. First of all, you played two ways up to 1950. Then you had to put the ball carrier down. Another thing, forearms were legal."

Bucko Kilroy, still active at 81 as a consultant with the Super Bowl champion New England Patriots, played offensive guard and middle guard on defense for the Eagles during their greatest era. He was an All-Pro on both sides of the ball, nasty and relentless in his style. He now laughs at, but won't reveal, the number of opponents he knocked out in his time. "Oh yeah," laughed Kilroy. "That happened when you blindsided a guy and he didn't see you coming. It was perfectly legal. But they checked me out pretty good in the films."

According to Kilroy, Washington Redskins executive Dick McCann got so frustrated with the victims of Bucko's menacing forearms that he came right out with it. "They should be bronzed," he said. Who could blame McCann? In the 13 years that Kilroy was tossing his weight, and his forearms, around, the Redskins defeated the Eagles only seven times. Yet Bucko insists he was

21

Bucko Kilroy, shown above as an Eagles assistant coach in 1960, is known as one of the toughest Eagles of all time. Now in his eighties, Kilroy works as a consultant to the New England Patriots.

ejected and fined only once, for kicking Ray Bray, a Chicago Bears guard. Like the Eagles, the Bears were a team of alley-fighters. "It was a preseason game," Bucko recalled. "I got hit in the back and was on the ground. So I kicked my leg upwards and got him. I got him in the right place."

In Kilroy's era, it was all power and muscle. The Eagles featured Steve Van Buren, one of the league's few power-and-speed backs. The game plan could have been scratched on a vacation postcard from Atlantic City. They gave the ball to Van Buren and cleared everybody out of the way. Or they ran Van Buren wide and, as Kilroy said, cleared out the pursuit with those nasty blind-side blocks, swinging their forearms through the air. "Oh, they were tough, very tough," said Bucko of his old team. "They were very physical. A couple of opposing players told me later that half of all their guys would come up with pulled muscles before our game."

Kilroy lined up at right guard on offense. After the Eagles punted, he played middle guard. But the middle guard spot was far different than the modern middle guard, also known as a nose tackle. "The middle guard very seldom crossed the line of scrimmage," said Kilroy. "Most of the time he was in pass coverage. Weak side zone, strong side zone, or man-to-man on the fullback." Bucko would drop and cover. Then the defense would simply huddle on offense, sometimes gasping for breath after a long series. It was a tough, grinding game played in baseball stadiums with wooden bleachers and chopped-up grass fields. "If you made $10,000, you were doing pretty good," he said. "Seventy-five hundred was the average. We didn't play for money. We played for fun."

Kilroy credits legendary Bears owner and coach George Halas for taking pro football out of the hard-knocks era. "Not everyone gives him credit for it," he said, "but Halas was the guy that made pro football. He brought the T-formation in and made it a spectator sport. Everybody had to fall in line and copy what he did. Before that, everybody banged it out. Run...run...run...run. It almost sounded like a cricket. Most of the T-formation quarterbacks were tailbacks in college. [Bob] Waterfield at USC. [Norm] Van Brocklin at Oregon. Even Sammy Baugh at TCU. Up until '47, there were only two T-formation teams, the Bears and the Eagles. You have to be 80 years old to remember these things."

Bucko Kilroy turned 81 on May 30, 2002. After his playing career ended, he continued his remarkable association with pro football as a coach, personnel director, general manager, vice president, and, since 1994, as a consultant. The last 32 years of his 60-year career that followed his retirement as the toughest Eagle of his day have been with the Patriots, Bucko's adopted team.

He loves to reminisce, or talk about the draft ratings, using a system to evaluate prospects that he originated. Yet Bucko was reluctant to discuss a story in *Life* magazine about the game's dirtiest players. He was labeled an "ornery critter," according to the league's official encyclopedia that named Kilroy one of the game's top 300 players. Bucko won't go into the legal details, other than to say he sued and he won.

HAROLD CARMICHAEL

Up until Ozzie Newsome broke his streak of 127 straight games with a pass reception, Harold Carmichael was the king of the streakers. He broke Dan Abramowicz's record of 105 consecutive games in 1979 and was rewarded with the ultimate bauble: a gleaming, towering trophy that measured 23 feet, nine inches from base to tip. It might have seemed excessively huge, meant for the *Guiness Book of World Records*. But for the six-foot-eight Carmichael, it seemed fitting.

Carmichael was a cornerback's agony. Aside from his height, his hands from palm to middle finger measured nine and a half inches. His arms extended 39 inches. He was a flamboyant figure off the field, driving a red Coupe deVille with opera windows the shape of footballs. His end zone celebrations were just as fancy. Carmichael would spin a football, and then he, Charlie Smith, and Don Zimmerman would extend their hands, as if rolling dice.

There were critics who thought of Carmichael as just another tall receiver, who beat those little five-foot-eight corners with his height advantage. Indeed, as a rookie Carmichael used to hear it from Tom Fears, the receivers coach. "Those little guys owned Carmichael," Fears would say. "He'd telegraph his moves, just like a boxer telegraphs his punches. They'd beat him to the spot."

But Carmichael, who played at Southern University, never had the game broken down for him. "I had a problem with cutting," he said. "They found I wasn't keeping my weight over my feet. That was causing me to slip." The city's boo-birds used him as a convenient target, calling him a hot dog. "I think the writers told them that," said Carmichael. "I wasn't doggin' it. The reason I got that reputation was that I dropped a couple of balls. And that was at a time when we weren't winning."

Carmichael eventually got it right. During his streak, he played with five different quarterbacks: John Reaves, Pete Liske, Mike Boryla, Roman Gabriel, and Ron Jaworski. When Gabriel played, Carmichael was joined by 6'4½" Charle Young, a pass-catching tight end, and 6'4" flanker Don Zimmerman. They came to be known as the "Fire High Gang." But it would be a mistake to think that Harold Carmichael developed into a Pro Bowl receiver strictly because of his height advantage.

"He was just a super receiver," said Jaworski. "For a guy his height, he's not just a tall guy. He's got flexibility...quick feet...he can make catches behind him that a quick five-foot-eight guy couldn't. He's a real athlete."

Carmichael loved those years with Young and Zimmerman, when every Sunday was a passing clinic because the Eagles lacked a star back. "You knew you were going to be doing a lot of passing, and you knew they couldn't always double you. 'Cause Charle would burn 'em and Zim would burn 'em."

Years later, the Eagles hired Carmichael as their director of player relations. He had played 13 seasons as the team's go-to receiver and caught 590 passes, all but one as an Eagle. "I had a rookie in here, a guy they were thinking about drafting," Carmichael said. "I walked with him to the cafeteria and we passed by my picture. I said, 'That's me.'" Carmichael, a former high school quarterback in Jacksonville, Florida, was shown tossing an end-around pass. The rookie seemed surprised. "Yeah, I threw a pass in a game, a touchdown pass," he said. "I could even throw the ball 105 yards." The rookie was startled. "One hundred and five yards?" he blurted. "Gosh, I've never heard of anybody throwing that far."

Indeed Carmichael could zoom them that far, noting that "they used to use me as a JUGS machine on kickoff return drills. I could place the ball wherever they wanted. But I couldn't throw it five yards now. My rotator cuff is totally ripped up."

As for that 23-foot trophy that was placed in the Hall of Fame, Carmichael says he owns a six-foot replica of the original. "I was there for Tommy McDonald's induction, and I didn't see it," he said. "They said the trophy had been taken down during some renovation and it had toppled over. I don't know what happened to it."

JEROME BROWN

His life ended at 27 behind the wheel of a very fast sports car. Jerome Brown couldn't control his new Corvette, which struck a utility pole on a rain-slick highway in rural Brooksville, Florida, killing him instantly. He wasn't the best defensive tackle to ever play for the Eagles, since his career lasted only five seasons. But he might have been had he lived.

Brown was a huge athlete, 6-foo-3 and easily 300 pounds. He had quick feet and powerful arms, and he could punish blockers in order to punish runners. "He was the best defensive lineman in the league," said his coach, Buddy Ryan. "He wound the defense up on game day." Brown was also a dressing-room clown who cursed, sang (usually in a falsetto voice), whistled, and loved to intimidate reporters with his insulting wit.

"He was a good guy, loud and boisterous but caring," said former club president Harry Gamble. "He loved to drive fast cars," said Mike Golic, Brown's linemate. "He lived fast and he drove fast. That was Jerome."

Under Ryan, the Eagles fielded a defense that played with a high sense of disdain. In 1991, Brown's last season, the Eagles were regarded as the league's best defense and easily the most intimidating. The rush line included Brown, either Golic or Mike Pitts inside, and Reggie White and Clyde Simmons outside. Brown accounted for 150 tackles and made the Pro Bowl.

Brown dressed next to White, an ordained minister known as the Minister of Defense. After games, Brown would begin to swear and sing, ignoring that White was indeed a man of the cloth. "I'm going out tonight and I'm going to get it," Brown would sing. "I'm going to get what I want and you reporters aren't invited."

When somebody once began discussing the major-league playoffs, Brown found a sack of oranges and began tossing them against a back wall. A slider here...a sinker there...a fastball. "He was the team's personality," said Golic. "He kept that room loose."

In the off-season, Brown turned to others in need. He ran a camp for underprivileged kids. One year he helped a Brooksville native pay for hospital bills after his 11-year-old daughter was left in a coma from an auto accident. "He did things that people didn't know about," said former teammate Keith Jackson. "He had a big heart. He was a different person behind the scenes."

In Philadelphia, they still remember Brown's devilish smile and his line on life. "My personality is to have fun," he once said. Even at such a young age, that smile made him seem like a man to whom every adventure in life had already happened. Or was about to happen, when he lost everything on that slick country road on June 25, 1992. He might have been the best inside lineman to ever play for the Eagles. He and Reggie White might have been the best left side of any four-man line in pro football history. But we will never know. "He had a heart for people," said Reggie White of his dear friend. A year later, White was gone, too, off to Green Bay to win a Super Bowl.

WILBERT MONTGOMERY

Gladys Montgomery, a woman of good sense, never wanted any of her sons to play football. The way she figured, it was like fighting. And since all of her seven sons were running backs, she figured, too, that they would always take more punishment than they would give.

"She told me it was craziness, a lot of fools ripping each other's arms and legs off," said Wilbert Montgomery, the best of the running brothers. "My older brother separated both shoulders playing in junior college, and my mother swore none of her sons would ever play football again."

Wilbert Montgomery got away with it by telling tall stories about hanging out or having sleepovers with friends. He became a great high school back, and with his mother's grudging approval, he earned a scholarship to Abilene Christian. Montgomery scored 76 touchdowns for Abilene, 37 in his freshman year alone. But there were injuries: a dislocated shoulder, followed by a bruised shoulder, followed by a bruised thigh, in which a calcium deposit developed.

Montgomery flunked a predraft physical with the New England Patriots when the doctors took a dim view of his injured thigh. But an Eagles scout named Bill Baker believed in his potential. The Eagles listened to Baker's pitch and took Montgomery as a sixth-rounder in the 1977 draft, figuring he was fast enough to return kicks and maybe develop into a third-down specialist.

But soon Montgomery was showing them a burst and a wiggle, just as he did at Abilene. He rushed for 1,220 yards and 1,512 yards in his second and third years. His career total of 6,538 yards wiped out Steve Van Buren's 33-year-old record. "You're within the top three backs in the league," Van Buren told Montgomery. "Actually, you and [Walter] Payton are the best."

Luck is always a part of stunning draft picks, and the Eagles got lucky when they took Montgomery out of the hands of the New England medics. Predictably, all of the strategists who were in the Eagles' war room that year swear they knew he was the sleeper of the 1977 draft. In retrospect, Wilbert Montgomery was probably the best draft pick ever made by the Eagles. He was more than just a gifted back. Shy, even retiring, Montgomery loved to hang around the dressing room after workouts. "Just sit around and shoot the bull, mess around with Otho [trainer Otho Davis] till the traffic dies down after practice," he used to say.

Montgomery was so good and so natural that he could have earned a nice off-season bonus by signing autographs at suburban malls and endorsing health products. Instead, he opted to rent a modest apartment in Abilene...without a phone. In effect, he was out of touch with his mother, his head coach, Dick Vermeil, and his agent, Robert MacDonald.

"Of all my children, I was probably closest to Wilbert," said Gladys Montgomery. "He stayed around the house more than the others. He'd sit with me while I cooked the dinner. He was a wonderful influence on his younger brothers. I still remember the day he left for Abilene. Lord, how the two of us cried."

Don't think for a fast minute that Montgomery was a mamma's boy. During his second season, there was a rumble along Pattison Avenue, not far from Veterans Stadium. Montgomery and teammates Billy Campfield and Oren Middlebrook were driving home after a Phillies playoff game. "There were seven guys in another car," said Montgomery. "They began throwing beer cans at us. We came to a stoplight and one of the guys jumped on the back of our car and started beating on the trunk."

Montgomery decked two of the antagonists. Campfield and Middlebrook won their hand fights, too, before the police arrived to halt the gutter fights. "They said those guys picked on the wrong guys," said Montgomery. The toughness of the man didn't surprise the late Jackie Graves, the assistant director of personnel. "Everybody looks at Wilbert and thinks he's too little," said Graves. "He's short, not small. He's well put together. He's got great strength in his legs and upper body. There were small things he was doing wrong, but he was doing them with great intensity."

Montgomery drifted to the Detroit Lions in 1985 following a contract dispute. The heart for the game was still there, but the injuries that Gladys Montgomery always feared had taken away his burst to the hole. He rushed

A sixth-round draft pick in 1977, Wilbert Montgomery developed into a force in the Eagles backfield, totaling 6,538 yards in his Eagles career.

for 251 yards, continuing a downward slide, and then he was out of the game.

When his old coach, Dick Vermeil, returned as head coach of the St. Louis Rams in 1997, he hired Montgomery as one of his assistants. Vermeil couldn't shake the very special bond between him and his back.

BILL BERGEY

Bill Bergey looked like a linebacker was supposed to look. Thick body, the arms of a weightlifter who had been doing curls all his life, wide shoulders and toes that pointed slightly inward in his walk, suggesting speed when he ran. But at Arkansas State, Bergey was considered anything but a linebacker.

"When I went to college, I was a fullback," said Bergey. "The players at Arkansas State laughed at me becoming a fullback there. They started me out as an offensive lineman. That didn't work. Then they tried me on defense at the nose guard position."

By the time he was a junior, Bergey had been shuffled back and forth as a spot player. Then a wise coach named Benny Ellender came to him one day and said, "Bill, you've got speed. You've got the size. We're going to make you a linebacker."

It was a sudden fit. Bergey married his new position, He became the greatest linebacker in Arkansas State history and developed into a Pro Bowl middle linebacker with the Eagles. "With my God-given talent, I just maxed it," he said.

He was tough and quick into the running hole. He was as fast as Chicago's Brian Urlacher and as relentless as Baltimore's Ray Lewis. If he had played today, he might have been the league's first $5 million backer. "I always thought he was greatly underrated," said Mike McCormack, who made the deal with Cincinnati for Bergey in 1974. The Bengals knew they were getting an aggressive playmaker when they drafted Bergey. But they didn't figure it would spill over to the negotiating table.

"Paul Brown offered me $16,000, $17,500, and $19,000, with a $5,000 bonus, on a three-year contract," said Bergey. "Then came three of the longest months of my life." After the holdout, Bergey cut a deal for $18,000, $20,000, and $22,000, with a $10,000 bonus. "I showed Paul Brown who was boss," he said.

But Brown showed Bergey the door in a 1974 trade forced on the Bengals by hard-line economics. In Philadelphia, Bergey became the leader of a 3-4

A four-time Pro Bowler, Bill Bergey was the leader of a 3-4 defense that terrorized the NFC East in the late 1970s.

defense that terrorized the NFC East. "We were like the four musketeers," said Bergey. "All for one and one for all." With Bergey and Frank LeMaster inside and John Bunting and Jerry Robinson outside, the Eagles flowed in waves to the ball and brought the city its first Super Bowl in 1980. The Eagles backers were so dedicated that they often spent Wednesday nights at a Holiday Inn adjacent to Veterans Stadium, mirroring their coach, Dick Vermeil.

But by then, Bergey was slipping. He had blown out his knee early in the 1979 season. "If at one time I was a 100-percent football player, I was only 65 percent after the knee," he said. "In '80 and '81, those seasons when we went to the Super Bowl, it just wasn't the same. The thing that stands out was our conference championship game. When we came down that ramp, it was 100 percent. No one thought we were not going to win that game. The score was 20-7. But that wasn't indicative of the way the game went. We really annihilated the Dallas Cowboys. We had Danny White talking out the side of his helmet. The Super Bowl was almost like an afterthought. It just wasn't the same as the conference game."

When Bill Bergey thinks back on his Eagle career, he doesn't dwell on the Super Bowl loss to the Oakland Raiders. Or the fact that some of today's punters earn more than he did as a four-time Pro Bowler. "I got a taste of it," he says. "I just like to see guys give a top performance out there. Look at Warren Sapp. He didn't have an individual tackle against the Philadelphia Eagles in that playoff. And Randy Moss in Minnesota with his attitude. That's the kind of stuff that bothers me."

BILL BRADLEY

In Palestine, Texas, Bill Bradley is remembered as a schoolboy legend who could run, throw, catch, tackle, punt, and return punts. The great Doak Walker once suggested while Bradley was practicing at SMU for an all-star game that he "probably had a big red 'S' underneath on his T-shirt." Thus was born the legend of Super Bill Bradley, or just Super Bill in the huddle.

Bradley and Jerry Levias, a little wide receiver and a Texas legend in his own right, came together in the summer of 1964 when they were high school all-stars. "Coming out of high school, the state was still segregated," said Bradley. "They hadn't even integrated the school system. There were three big all-star games. They put us up at SMU, and the guy running the game asked me if I would mind rooming with Jerry Levias. I didn't have any photo of him, so I got curious and asked him why he bothered to ask."

"He's a black player," the man said.

"Well, he's a football player, isn't he?" said Bradley.

They got along like brothers. Indeed, after playing together in all three all-star games, Levias began referring to Bradley as his "blue-eyed soul brother." In the second game, pitting Texas against Pennsylvania, all-star coach Bobby Layne waved Bradley into the game as a quarterback, one of his skill positions. "Jerry wasn't very big," said Bradley, "but I just lofted the ball up in the air and he'd catch it. From then on, I was his 'blue-eyed soul brother.' It kind of stuck with me."

Bradley played eight years for the Eagles after a superstar career at the University of Texas. He was a great free safety, intercepting 20 passes in 1971-72. Super Bill also punted, returned punts and kickoffs, and held on field goals. His tackling was so aggressive that no less a figure than Dallas coach Tom Landry once called him "Cheap-Shot Bill."

The legend continues in Texas. But in Philadelphia, Bradley is remembered best for an improbable 17-day training camp holdout in which he and linebacker Tim Rossovich roamed the beaches along the Jersey shore. They were like movie stars, changing hotels and workout locations to avoid the sports paparazzi. "It was a cops-and-robbers deal," said Bradley. There were numerous sightings, but the photogs could never spot either player.

"The *Inquirer* ran a half-page layout of a huge dollar bill with a picture of Timmy in place of George Washington," said Bradley. "We stayed in Margate and Avalon. Every day we'd pick out a spot on the beach to work out. Even if the sand was soft, you could work your calves. Then we'd hang out in Maloney's bar down in Avalon. Timmy was serious about workouts. When we got back, I was in the best shape I'd ever been in."

The Eagles ended the Bradley-Rossovich caper by trading the eccentric Rossovich to San Diego. Bradley went on to play eight years for the Eagles. His legend never grew because the Eagles struggled through seven losing seasons and a 7-7 standoff in 1974. Bradley walked off the field a winner only twice in 16 games against the rival Cowboys.

"Yeah, there was a little bit of a vendetta there," Bradley said. "The Cowboys would contact you and work you out and tell you they were going to draft you. In my case, they said they were going to draft me in the second round. But they didn't."

Blackie Sherrod, a Dallas writer, once asked Bradley if he ever wanted to play for Tom Landry.

"Oh, no," said Bradley. "I never, never wanted to play for Tom Landry. His britches were too tight."

TIMMY BROWN

Dr. James Nixon, the Eagles physician, once observed that Timmy Brown had the most perfectly sculpted body of any athlete he had ever examined. Brown was well-muscled; extremely shifty and fast. During his eight-year career with the Eagles, he was also the best pass-catching back in pro football.

So why isn't Timmy Brown in the Hall of Fame? And why doesn't he hold any of the 13 rushing records in the Eagle books? Moreover, why does he look back on his career with more than a trace of bitterness?

Brown was the Marshall Faulk of his era. "I had a great career with the Eagles until [Joe] Kuharich came," he said. "Joe made up his mind that he was going to bend and break my spirit. I was jovial. He didn't like that."

The first team meeting attended by the breakaway back, who had been waived in 1960 by the Green Bay Packers, and the eccentric head coach was filled with cutting lines. Brown had been in ROTC training for several weeks. He promptly pulled a hamstring muscle on the first day of training, a nagging injury throughout Brown's career.

"We're not going to have any stars on this team," Kuharich said in his pep speech to the Eagles. "Do you have a problem with that, Mr. Brown?"

Brown burned deep inside. "Would you repeat that again, sir?" he said.

"I said, 'Do you have a problem with that, Mr. Brown?'"

Brown paused for just the right effect. "The only time I think that way is if you don't give me the ball," he said. "And you know what, he took that to heart."

According to Brown, Kuharich purposely avoided calling his number. Brown remembers two games in the 1965 season. Bob Brown, the massive tackle, and Pro Bowl center Jim Ringo were cutting up the Browns in the trenches, and Timmy Brown was making all the right blocking reads. He rushed for 186 yards but got only 16 carries against the Cardinals. Against the Browns, Brown's first-half rushing total was a staggering 169 yards. Steve Van Buren's club record of 205 yards (that still stands after 53 years) appeared doomed. But then Brown had only four carries in the second half and took a helmet in the ribs, missing the entire fourth period.

Timmy Brown was a skilled pass-catcher with speed and a perfectly sculpted body, but he could never get out of head coach Joe Kuharich's doghouse.

"Jim Brown had the league record of 232 yards," said Brown. "Jim Ringo and Bob Brown, they were excited. I said to them, 'Let's do it.' Later, everybody was saying, 'What happened to Timmy?'" Years later, Brown's response is that he played for a coach who didn't believe in the star system.

In 1966, Brown was so deep in Kuharich's doghouse that he was begging for playing time. "I wanted to play wide receiver," he said. "I wanted to play defense. I wanted to play 60 minutes." They finally waved Timmy Brown out with the kickoff return team in a midseason game against Dallas. Brown broke not one but two returns for touchdowns. The dazzling plays covered 90 and 93 yards. Two angry years later, he was playing for the Baltimore Colts.

"I feel very unfulfilled in football," Brown now says. "My four years with Kuharich were just a waste. He was determined to break me. Hey, Joe never had a winning record except in college at San Francisco. I could never play for him. I hated the guy with a passion."

Despite the anger and frustration, Brown also must feel the intense pride that comes with the long climb he made from an uncertain childhood. He spent five years in two different foster homes. He graduated at 17 from the Soldiers and Sailors Children's Home in Indiana. Then he earned a basketball scholarship to Ball State that evolved into a football career.

Timmy Brown is now a probation officer in Los Angeles, working with adults under "the military aspect" of life. He made a decent, if unpredictable, living as an actor for 25 years. "I spoke my mind," he said. "They liked 'yes' men. They found excuses not to use me." It was almost as if old Joe Kuharich was sitting in the director's chair.

And how does Timmy Brown reflect on his playing years? "I had a great time in Philadelphia," he said. "I was never booed and they're known for booing. I really felt loved there and I really loved Philadelphia. I was very insecure because of my background. I kept people at arm's length, so I wouldn't hurt anyone."

TOMMY McDONALD

They weep, they laugh, and sometimes they stumble over the words on that very special summer day on the famous rotunda at the Pro Football Hall of Fame in Canton, Ohio. Tommy McDonald, the most exciting receiver in Eagles history, left them laughing during his rousing induction speech in 1998. Now McDonald will leave them stunned with the admission that his

Despite his 5-foot-9 stature, Tommy McDonald came up big with the ball in his hands, scoring 84 career touchdowns.

selection to the Hall of Fame wasn't the most important thing to happen in his 13-year-career.

"Don Hutson and Dan Currie once told me that when the Packers watched films of the Eagles, Vince Lombardi always talked about me," said McDonald. "They said Lombardi used to say, 'How come we don't have any receiver like that McDonald kid? If I had 11 Tommy McDonalds, we'd win the championship every year.' That was the greatest thing to happen to me. [Lombardi] never threw flowers at anybody."

Lombardi marveled at the way McDonald wove his way into the end zone after a catch. "Every fifth ball went for a touchdown," McDonald said. "The quarterbacks, [Sonny] Jurgensen and Norm Van Brocklin, they'd say, 'That little squirt is going to get the ball in the end zone.'" McDonald scored 84 touchdowns in his career, trailing only Hutson (99) and Paul Warfield (85). Yet he stood only five foot nine and weighed only 165 pounds when he reported to the Eagles. "I'm the shortest guy to go into the Hall of Fame," he said. "I wasn't real fast, either. I ran 40 yards in 4.6 seconds. What I was really good at was changing direction. Getting to a spot real fast, like you do in racquetball or tennis."

Some receivers are trash-talkers, babbling away at cornerbacks to win the mind games they play. Tommy McDonald, however, raves about the corners he knew. Actually, he almost became one of them. After his career ended in 1968, McDonald began plotting a comeback...on the defensive side of the ball.

"I was seriously thinking about going back as a defensive halfback," he said. "A couple of times I almost picked up the phone to call Vince Lombardi down at Washington. See, I appreciated the defensive side of it. I always admired a lot of people who were defensive backs. You've almost got to be a better athlete than a receiver has to be. Receivers know where they're going. The defensive back has got to anticipate where they're going. He has to have great speed when facing a real grass-burner like Bob Hayes."

McDonald played both ways at Oklahoma. He was an elusive halfback in Bud Wilkinson's split-T attack, then flopped to the secondary on defense. The Eagles, however, were loaded with backs: Clarence Peaks, Billy Ray Barnes, Ken Keller, and Skippy Minisi. When wideout Bill Stribling pulled a leg muscle, receivers coach Charley Gauer remembered how smooth and easy McDonald caught passes from Sooners teammate Jimmy Harris in predraft workouts at Norman, Oklahoma. In his first start against the Washington Redskins, McDonald ran to the spots and caught touchdown passes of 61 and 25 yards.

"I think we've found a spot for you," kidded Gauer. McDonald admits he never could have survived as a 165-pound back. "No, no," he said. "I'm not that type of running back. In the NFL, you've got to be a player who lowers his head to make another half-yard, or two yards when you get hit. When I got hit, I'm so little I'm not going to run over anybody. Now, could I have made it as a defensive halfback? Absolutely, sure. I liked defense better than offense."

PETE RETZLAFF

South Dakota State was out there somewhere in the far, far west. But even if the scouts had a map and a reason, they ignored the school where Pete Retzlaff starred in football and threw the discus. Once the scouts evaluated the prospects from the major schools, it became a guessing game for the leftovers.

"Most of the teams concentrated on Division I football," said Retzlaff. "You look back into the history of it, the top players every year came out of Division I schools. The scouting departments weren't very well organized, in the sense that a lot of professional teams subscribed to college newspapers. They'd read about all of the football statistics, and when somebody did something that was impressive, they took an interest. I got a letter from the Bears at the same time Detroit seemed to be interested in me. The letter said, 'If you're not drafted, let us know and come in as a free agent.'"

Retzlaff was drafted by the Lions in the 22nd round of the 1956 draft. He got a handshake and a $5,000 contract as a fullback prospect from way out west. "I just tried to stay alive," said Retzlaff. "When you're the 22d draft choice, you're not exactly looked upon as an impact player."

A few days before he was cut, Retzlaff was walking off the field with Doak Walker, the great Lions back. "Look, Pete," Walker said, "there are several of us here who think you have the talent to make it in the NFL."

The Lions should have listened to Walker's evaluation. The Eagles were loaded with backs, including Ted Dean, Clarence Peaks, Tommy McDonald, Billy Ray Barnes, and Ken Keller. Out of necessity, the Eagles flopped Retzlaff to wide receiver. But then tight end Bobby Walston broke his arm. "It was either me or McDonald who was going to play," said Retzlaff. "I think that choice was fairly obvious."

McDonald, drafted as a 165-pound back, became a Pro Bowl receiver. Retzlaff, a small-school fullback, became the best tight end in Eagles history. So much for the NFL's primitive scouting system. "Under Buck Shaw," said Retzlaff, "every receiver had to know every other receiver's assignments. The two running backs as well as the three receivers. He wanted them to be interchangeable."

An unknown coming out of South Dakota State, Pete Retzlaff switched positions from fullback and became the best tight end in Eagles history.

"The Baron," as Retzlaff was known for his commanding physique and playing style, finished his career with 452 catches, 47 touchdowns, and a championship ring. He could have played a few more seasons but retired in 1966 to start a career in broadcasting.

"I didn't exactly see eye to eye with Joe Kuharich," he said. "But in my 11th year, after about a week of two-a-days, I could tell it was not where my heart was. I gave it everything I could. On every play you've got a responsibility, regardless of who the coach is."

Retzlaff had a chance to jump to the AFL's Miami Dolphins during the premerger raiding years. The offer was for nearly $1 million. "They had contacted me about playing out my option," said Retzlaff. "But I had just re-signed two weeks before for $46,000. Timing is everything."

As Pete Retzlaff thought back to his college career and how the scouts never set foot on the South Dakota State campus, he remembered what Norm Van Brocklin once told him. "He said the Eagles used to draft from Look magazine," said Retzlaff. "They had these All-America teams, first, second, third and fourth teams, and that's how the Eagles drafted."

ROMAN GABRIEL

Even the name conjures up thoughts of a grand figure, majestic in size and presence. Roman Gabriel was all of that. He arrived in 1973 in another of those Los Angeles-to-Philadelphia quarterback trades, following Norm Van Brocklin and preceding Ron Jaworski. Gabriel's arm had gone bad the previous year, when he threw only 12 touchdown passes for a Rams team in decline.

He was 33 but he looked 23, rangy with a Malibu tan and a belief that Kung Fu was as necessary in his life as football. "You learn to control every part of your body before you try to control others," Gabriel would say. "In a medium-type workout, you would be on your feet four hours with no break. It's a beautiful art. All the Kung Fu punches come from circular movements out of a football stance. A good Kung Fu man has got to work harder than a karate man. You see, Kung Fu means work master."

Gabriel adopted his work ethic from his father. "My father's my hero," he said. "And I always tried to be like him. I remember there were only four Filipinos in the state of North Carolina, and they all worked for the Atlantic Coast Line railroad as cooks or waiters. He'd be home for one day and one night and then be gone for three days. When I wasn't in school, he'd take me on the train. I always remember how hard he worked. He never smoked, never drank, never owned a car or had a license. He always walked everywhere."

When Gabriel joined the Eagles, he brought along a martial arts expert named Gus Hoefling, who became the team's strength and flexibility coach. Soon a lot of Eagles were kicking and flexing and stretching. "When Gabe was with the Rams," recalled Hoefling, "he had some elbow problems. I started workouts with him, and he got better. When they traded him to the Eagles, I sort of came along. The martial arts workouts lasted a couple of hours. There was a lot of conditioning, a lot of stretching. I remember him and Steve Zabel doing 1,500 sit-ups."

Yet for all of their unique motions, the Eagles never produced a winning season with Roman Gabriel under center. In 1973, Gabriel was the NFL's best quarterback, throwing for 23 touchdowns and a league-high 3,219 yards. Gabriel's offense, however, included too many slow-foots. Or what coaches called lard-asses. Over Gabriel's five seasons, the Eagles never had a 1,000-yard rusher. The offense, with Gabriel throwing to 6'8" Harold Carmichael, 6'4" Charle Young, and 6'3" Don Zimmerman, known collectively as the Fire High Gang, scored 30 or more points only four times. In the Gabriel years, the Eagles lost 16 games by seven or fewer points and 10 by four points or less.

Gabriel was eventually benched in 1976, and then Jaworski arrived to start a new era. Hoefling moved to the Phillies. Yet Roman Gabriel remains a quarterback to remember. He attacked the Kung Fu drills and used a mystical balm created by a New York woman on his ailing elbow. He left the game in 1977 after 16 years without a Super Bowl ring. But he had his own individual championship, the lord of the sweat.

AL WISTERT

They were weary and rain-soaked but laughing and hugging each other, the tears of joy mixing with the raindrops. They had just won their second straight NFL championship in 1949, shutting out the Los Angeles Rams 14-0 in the muddy Coliseum, their eighth shutout in two years.

"Suddenly it dawned on us that we've got to do something to commemorate the game," said Al Wistert, the two-way tackle. "Our fullback, Joe Muha, designed a ring. It was quite a nice design. We got it priced, and you could buy it for $65. We put in an order, but some of the guys didn't think they could afford $65. That's how things were in those days. I guess about 70 percent of the guys ordered the ring. It didn't even have a diamond in it. I gave mine to my grandson when he graduated from the police academy. Mine had a diamond in it. It came out of the wedding ring from my sister Belle."

The Eagles never gave a thought about buying rings or watches for their heroes. Not in the early years of pro football, when the gates were poor and there were no television revenues. They did host a postgame party at the swank Bel Air Country Club. The expenses, however, came out of the game receipts. "It was a very exclusive spot, right near the UCLA campus," recalled Wistert. "They held a dinner banquet for us. As part of the commemoration for winning the championship, they gave us these Zippo cigarette lighters. They probably cost 98 cents, at a quantity cost. They didn't even have our names on them, or anything else about the championship. I left mine at the table."

Al Wistert is now 81. He lives on a woodsy five-acre plot in Grands Pass, Oregon, about 90 miles from the California border and a mile from the scenic Rogue River, ("the best salmon in the whole territory," says Wistert). Kathy Wistert's 46-year-old daughter still lives with her family. "She is handicapped," says Wistert. "She was born without a thyroid gland. She loves horses. She has nine of them that were abused or neglected."

In the '40s, players rarely left the field. They just regrouped, offense flopping to defense, or the other way around. Al Wistert was a two-way tackle. "I played both ways, 60 minutes, in college," he said. "With the Eagles, it was the same way, 60 minutes."

Wistert remembers limping off the field during a game.

"What's the matter, Al?" said Coach Greasy Neale. "What's the matter?"

"I think I've broken my leg," said Wistert, grimacing.

"Get back in there till you're sure," said Neale, turning away.

Wistert would open the season as a 215-pound tackle. In 1946, after a particularly tough opener against the Rams, he lost 16 pounds, dropping below 200. "I played at 198 the rest of the season," he said. "And I still made All-Pro."

They were an older, tougher team. Many of the Eagles had just gotten out of the service when they came together to form what Wistert calls "the greatest team the Eagles ever had." As fellow tackle Bucko Kilroy has said, referring to Pete Pihos, Chuck Bednarik, Joe Muha, Tommy Thompson, and all the other military heroes who returned to the game, "After they taught you to kill, none of these fellows ever backed down."

"The guys came back out of the service, and the team started to build under Greasy Neale," said Wistert. "Lex Thompson was the owner. He was a Yale grad, and Greasy had been invited to help out as an assistant coach at Yale. If you knew Greasy, he was a tough cob."

Ironically, Wistert never played football in high school. Instead, he hung around the sandlots and parks in Chicago, learning the game from older youths. "They had an excellent athletic program in the public parks," he said. "That's where I learned, in those parks."

Wistert still dreams about being selected to the Hall of Fame for his superb play in the trenches over a nine-year pro career. "I sure would like to be in there," he said wistfully.

BOB BROWN

Willie Davis, Green Bay's Hall of Fame defensive end, once gave this advice to Bob Brown. "Bob," said Davis, "play on Sunday so you can look at yourself and live with yourself on Monday." As a Cleveland schoolboy, Brown had met Davis when he played for the Browns. Ironically, they later played against each other after Davis joined the Packers.

Brown lived by Davis' motto through a dominating 10-year career in which he was a Pro Bowler with three different teams and offensive lineman of the year in 1970. "I wasn't fancy," said Brown. "I was the first 300-pounder who was quick and could move. I tried to be physical and make you feel pain. I was like a 60-pound sledgehammer when I played."

Brown was so big and so good that he could clear the entire side of a defensive line with his enormous size, power, and quickness. Which brings up a question that has haunted Bob Brown for years. Why isn't he a member of Pro Football's Hall of Fame? Brown has been nominated three times. But each time he has fallen short of votes, perhaps because he was an Eagle for five years, a Los Angeles Ram for two years, and an Oakland Raider for three years. In those years, there was almost a stigma attached to the movers of the league.

"I'm extremely disappointed; I am," said Brown. "I wouldn't be honest if I said it didn't matter. I played 10 years. I was All-Pro seven or eight. That's not bad. Yes, I'm disappointed. It's not so much that I need the acclaim. I didn't play for that. But just ask Deacon Jones. Call Claude Humphrey. Call

Carl Eller. Ask them who would they rate as the toughest to block. I think I'm going to be there when they answer. I don't know. Maybe I'm not supposed to be in there. Maybe I slipped through the cracks. I don't know if I believe in destiny or not. I know I'm not sitting around sucking my thumb and pining about it."

Brown was the Eagles' first draft choice in 1964, the same year that Joe Kuharich was hired as head coach. His line coach was Dick Stanfel, a brilliant tactician and motivator. Kuharich's teams could score. But the defense was thin and slow. While Brown and Kuharich built a special bond, the Eagles never reached the playoffs. When Kuharich was fired after the 1968 season, Brown worked a protest trade to the Rams and left with him.

"I left because Joe was dealt with unfairly," Brown recalled. "With the Rams, George Allen was my coach. He liked a lot of rah-rah, and that was not my personality. I came to Oakland, and Al [Davis] and I had some differences. So I didn't have any one team with a sense of loyalty to me. I'm in flux. You mention the name of Bob Brown to some of the younger players today and they'll say, 'Bob who?'"

Brown was in a reflective mood. "I'm 60 years old," he said. "When I played, I wasn't beating up on women. I didn't do drugs. I wasn't into alcohol. I just came to work on Sunday."

And there was Stanfel, his Eagles coach. "The best line coach I ever knew," Brown said. "He knew all about line play. He knew how far you could reach block and when you could push the envelope a little bit."

Despite the disappointing years in Philadelphia, Brown still considers those seasons as rewarding, even special. "I had a great rapport with the fans," he said. "Those fans are the most knowledgeable in the league. But they can be very tough. I don't care if you're Allen Iverson. You play poorly and they're going to boo. They're going to boo Christ on the cross."

After all these years, Bob Brown can't shake the feeling that he belongs in Canton. "In my heart," he says, "I just believe that I'm deserving. I won't say entitled. Maybe they're ready to take another look."

Indeed, the Hall of Fame voters decided that this dominator, this huge man of muscle, quickness and leverage, deserved to be enshrined. Brown, who was better than Hall of Fame tackles Anthony Munoz and Ron Yary, was inducted in 2004. The honor that had escaped him was finally his.

MIKE QUICK

Just minutes before the Eagles were ready to draft a Clemson receiver named Perry Tuttle, they were ambushed by the Buffalo Bills. Trading up two first-round spots with Denver, from 21st to 19th, the Bills snatched Tuttle, leaving the Eagles to ponder what might have been.

But not for long. With Harold Carmichael and Charlie Smith at the ends of their careers, the Eagles in 1982 were desperate for a wide receiver. Even as general manager Carl Peterson was muttering about how Bills coach Chuck Knox had pulled a fast one on old friend Dick Vermeil, the Eagles took Mike Quick, a long-striding wideout from North Carolina State. "I remember at one of the combines I spent a lot of time with Coach Vermeil and his staff," said Quick. "Actually, I thought either the Saints or Browns were going to draft me. They showed the most interest. The interview with Coach Vermeil was a scary process. You're a wide-eyed kid getting his first shot in the pros. Then after getting off the plane from North Carolina, I remember all of these [TV] lights flashing in my eyes. I was kind of like a deer in the headlights. It was a little bit unsettling."

Drafts, as they say, take crazy twists. Tuttle, plagued by injuries, played only two years with the Bills. Lindsay Scott, the Saints' first-round receiver, lasted four years and was gone. Ah, but that Mike Quick. From 1983-86, he accounted for 42 touchdowns, or four out of every 10 touchdowns scored by the Eagles. In his brilliant nine-year career, Quick caught 363 passes, averaging 17.8 yards per catch and scoring 61 touchdowns.

"I was probably the most productive receiver in the league from '83 through those other years," said Quick. "I became the featured guy. I got a lot of opportunities. I caught the ball and made people miss. When we got close, a lot of times they'd throw to me. Even when they knew it was going to me, there was nothing they could do about it."

The highlight of Quick's career came when the Eagles were 99 yards away from the Atlanta end zone. "Mick Luckhurst had just missed a field goal," said Quick. "We went into overtime, and they ended up punting inside our one-yard line. I split the corner and safety and took off." Ron Jaworski delivered the ball as if they were filming for a clinic. Quick never broke stride and took it to the distant house, as they say, for the overtime win.

Quick made five Pro Bowl appearances. The one he remembers is the one he shouldn't remember. "That was awful," he said, referring to his third Pro Bowl after the 1986 season. "I was all excited about being in Hawaii. But I ended up eating some bad shellfish. I woke up at four in the morning, and I was losing everything. I called the trainer. But everything they gave me came right back up. I was too weak to play, so I sat in the dugout at one end of the field. It was shady there. I watched the game except when I was going back into the locker room. The next day, it was like nothing had ever happened."

Sure, the Eagles can now rave about drafting Mike Quick and how they really weren't interested in Perry Tuttle. The passing years, of course, dim the memory. But on the Eagles' draft board that day, it was Tuttle at the top, then Quick, then Scott. The Eagles simply got very, very lucky.

RANDALL CUNNINGHAM

In the 1985 predraft evaluation list, Randall Cunningham earned a 5.5 rating from the National Football Scouting Combine. He could throw the ball a long way, like John Elway. Maybe not as accurate, but certainly as forceful. And he could scramble better than Steve Young. But Cunningham was 6'4 ½" and weighed only 192 pounds, and he had a big windmill delivery that scared some scouts. So National rated him below Doug Flutie, Chuck Long, Steve Calabria, and Steve Bono. In his slot, he was categorized as a player with "above-average ability, better than a 50-50 chance to make an NFL squad." One team, the San Diego Chargers, rated him higher, but only as a punter who had averaged 47.5 yards at Nevada-Las Vegas.

Did he have the potential to develop? Or was he some scattershot passer like Reggie Collier, the USFL wonder blunder? Could somebody correct that windup, one that prompted the scouts to call him a windmiller?

Even today, 16 years after Randall Cunningham established himself as one of the most dangerous players in the game, his name opens a curious debate. When an unknowing secretary was asked if agent Jim Steiner still represented Cunningham, she was taken aback. "What is he?" she asked, as if Cunningham might be an NBA rebounder or a major-league outfielder. Former Eagles general manager Jim Murray had an answer. "He's a human highlight film," said Murray.

Ron Jaworski, Cunningham's predecessor, said a lot more. "If he would have been coached properly," said Jaworski, "he could have, or would have, been the greatest quarterback ever to play the game. He had more talent than anybody. He could throw the football. He had all the throws. You know. The stick throw on the deep comeback. The touch on the pass down the hole. The deep ball. Throwing the ball into the flat with accuracy. He was a young guy who needed to be coached. Doug Scovil was the coach who was bringing him along."

Scovil was Buddy Ryan's quarterback coach. He tightened Cunningham's delivery. He worked on footwork and Cunningham's follow-through. What developed was much more than a coach and a promising quarterback on the same page, as they say. This was as close to a father-son relationship as you could find outside the birth rolls. It was understandable, since Cunningham had lost both his parents when he was 18. And then Doug Scovil collapsed and died of a heart attack on December 9, 1989, and Cunningham lost him, too.

"I'm trying to get over it, but it isn't easy," Cunningham said at the time. "Sure, you care, but you don't want to dwell on it, or it will bother you for the rest of your life."

Without Scovil as his mentor, Cunningham reverted to some of his old habits. He was truly a big-play quarterback, producing those individual highlights that Jim Murray talked about. There was the stumbling touchdown pass, his hand actually touching down like an off-balance skater, against the New York Giants in 1988 on *Monday Night Football*. There was the scramble out of the end zone to elude Buffalo's Bruce Smith and find Fred Barnett on a 95-yard pass play in 1990. There was that bounding 91-yard punt against the New York Giants in 1989. Cunningham truly gave Philadelphia fans a lifetime of thrills. But he never gave them an NFC championship.

It really wasn't all Cunningham's fault. In his 11-year career in Philadelphia, the Eagles didn't send a single blocker or running back to the Pro Bowl. Indeed, Cunningham himself was the team's leading rusher from 1987-90. Those were the Buddy Ryan years, when Cunningham was told to go out and make some big plays and Ryan's defense would take care of business. Later, Cunningham would surface in Minnesota, Dallas, and Baltimore. In 1998 as a Viking, when he was tutored by Brian Billick, he threw 34 touchdown passes. He was 14-2 as a starter, falling one win short of a Super Bowl start.

"I'm very patient now," Cunningham said that year. "I can drop back and not worry about who is picked up and who isn't. I can look down the field, focus and fire. I used to drop back and have fear. Fear that I was going to be sacked. It's different now. I'm in the right place. I see the linemen coming forward, but I see a sense of peace, a sense of where the guys are going to be. I know when I can check one guy out or when I'm going to the third guy."

Randall Cunningham was a big-play quarterback who only harnessed his potential after moving on to the Minnesota Vikings.

Cunningham said that Billick was a lot like Doug Scovil, his early mentor. "When [Billick] came to visit me, God was saying, 'I'm moving you in a new direction, Randall,'" he said.

Back in Philadelphia, the fans are left to ponder what might have been if Scovil had lived and Randall Cunningham had matured, just as he finally did as a Viking. He was then 35, starting his 13th year. Ron Jaworski says he could have been the greatest of them all with proper coaching. But we will never know.

On Friday, August 23, 2002, before a preseason game between Philadelphia and the Baltimore Ravens, Cunningham officially retired as an Eagle.

"There is really nothing phony about Philadelphia, which is the thing I loved about it," he said. "In this life you go places where people have facades and people talk behind your back, but in Philadelphia everything was real. That's the thing I love about it."

SETH JOYNER

On January 31, 1999, more than 12 years after he was drafted as a suspect in the middle of the eighth round, linebacker Seth Joyner was a stranger in paradise. He walked into the balmy Florida night that year, knowing that he had finally earned a Super Bowl ring. He hadn't made a single big play, not even one tackle. He wore game jersey No. 99, colored in Denver blue and orange, the same number worn by Jerome Brown, his deceased Eagle teammate. On that day, his glory games behind him, Joyner ran all over the field with the Broncos' special teams.

"I wish it had been the previous year," said Joyner. "I was with Green Bay and started and played the whole game. It was a bittersweet year with Denver. It was the first time in my career that I wasn't a starter."

Actually, a Super Bowl should have come much earlier in Joyner's long career. He had beaten the odds as the 208th player drafted (the 29th linebacker) and worked his way onto Buddy Ryan's excellent defense that included Reggie White, the great pass rusher. Five years later, the unit had been joined by Jerome Brown, Byron Evans, Eric Allen, Clyde Simmons (an end drafted 25 spots lower than Joyner on the ninth round), and Wes Hopkins. That defense dominated across the board, finishing first against the run (71.0 yards per game) and pass (150.8) and allowing just 20 touchdowns. Yet the team faltered, losing four straight after quarterback Randall Cunningham suffered a season-ending knee injury in the opener.

"I always believed that we had a Super Bowl team in the making," said Joyner. "If [owner] Norman Braman had just let the team alone. If he had let Buddy do what he had to do. We had enough offensive weapons. It's just that the offensive line, we needed vast improvement there."

Joyner now can play a little game of what might have been if... (1) Cunningham had stayed healthy; (2) White had stayed with the defense instead of jumping to Green Bay; (3) Jerome Brown had not been killed in a car accident; and (4) Ryan had remained the head coach or coordinator Jeff Fisher and not Rich Kotite had succeeded him in 1991.

Before his eight-year career with the Eagles ended, Seth Joyner gave them two games for the ages. Late in that frustrating 1991 season, Joyner scored on a fumble return, forced another fumble that Simmons recovered for a touchdown, and caused another interception that set up yet another score. All of these heroics came in the first period against Phoenix. A week later, on *Monday Night Football*, Joyner forced two fumbles, recovered two, and added two sacks in another dazzling performance against Houston.

"Obviously, the high point of my career was having the opportunity to play in the Super Bowl," said Joyner, one of the Eagles' great draft picks. "The next was being able to play in Philadelphia. Those two games are memories. For me, they were huge games in terms of what it meant to the outcome of the game."

Joyner wants to be remembered as a player "who gave everything he had to give and had a genuine passion for being the best player he could be'." Like most former Eagles, he has a warm feeling for the city.

"The Philadelphia fans can be kind of rough at times," he said. "But even now when I go back, I still get a lot of love. Those years will always be etched in my mind. With those teams, we gave them some very, very exciting football games."

RON JAWORSKI

Other quarterbacks who have lost their form in the Super Bowl have returned home to be greeted like the city mayor who has cheated on the books. Ron Jaworski threw three interceptions during the painful loss in Super Bowl XV, all to the same Oakland defender. Yet he remains a popular figure, engaging and approachable, despite his clunker game against the

Raiders. "I think it's because I stayed here," said Jaworski. "I mean, I played the majority of my career here, 10 years, and for the most part, they were good years. And I think outside of football, I acclimated to this area and got involved with businesses and philanthropic organizations, the Eagles Fly for Leukemia and the United Way. I gave back to the community."

Jaworski also sees a real connection to his roots. "I grew up in Buffalo, and Philadelphia is very much to me like Buffalo. They are a hard-core, working-class type of people. I think I connected in that regard. I didn't always connect with them on the football field, but that's part of the way it goes."

Over the years, as a pocket quarterback without much mobility, Jaworski took all the tough hits without complaining. He once started 116 straight games, the equivalent of seven seasons. "I spent 21 years of my life in the steel mills and in steel towns, with lunch-bucket kinds of crowds," he said. "You know, the working stiffs would be a good way to put it. My family, my relatives, nieces and nephews, aunts and uncles, they were lunch-bucket people. They went to the mills and worked 40 hours a week. That's pretty much what I'd grown up to. Then all of a sudden, I'm out in Los Angeles, living in Marina del Rey. Oh, man. John Hadl lived across the street. I was just a kid from Youngstown State University. And now I was going to Tinseltown. It was different. Those fans sat on their hands. You'd look to see if Clint Eastwood was there."

Jaworski came to the Eagles in a 1977 trade. "I wasn't the most gifted guy to ever line up and play," he conceded. "But I always took great pride in my work ethic and toughness. I learned from Chuck Knox at a young age that no matter how much talent you have, if you're not tough enough to play with injuries and things, you're not helping your football team. I think the fans here, rather than any Super Bowl loss, they remember some of the good things I accomplished by lining up and playing every week."

Yet the Super Bowl defeat in the early hours of a grim New Orleans night still pains Ron Jaworski.

"It absolutely haunts me," he said. "I've looked at some of it. I mean, I've replayed the plays in my mind." His first interception came on his very first pass. "We had run that play 50-100 times that season," Jaworski said. "I could read that play in my sleep. But you get in a game like that and you try too hard. I should have dropped it off to Wilbert [Montgomery] in the flat and taken a three-yard gain. I tried to stick one in the seam to [tight end John Spagnola], and Rod Martin picked that one off."

Ron Jaworski, who threw three interceptions in the Eagles' Super Bowl XV loss to the Oakland Raiders, started 116 straight games at one point.

Jaworski says the postgame agony, once bearable, has increased with the passing years. "It's funny, but at the time it didn't sting as much because we really thought we were going to get back," he said. "We were a young team. We were disappointed, but we felt we were going to be back. We never got back. You get away from it, and now you say, 'Man, we had that one chance and we didn't take advantage of it.'"

When Ron Jaworski thinks back to the worst defeat of his hard-knocks career, he also thinks of the Eagles who were in his huddle. "It was a very special team," he said. "The most unique group of people I've ever been around." Herm Edwards, the cornerback, coaches the New York Jets. John Bunting, the linebacker, coaches at North Carolina. Guy Morriss, the center, coaches at Kentucky. Jerry Sisemore, the tackle, was a superintendent of schools in Texas. Montgomery, the back, coaches with the St. Louis Rams. Harold Carmichael, the 6-foot-8 receiver, is the Eagles' director of player relations.

"Dick Vermeil, our coach, taught us a lot more than being good football players," he said. "There are a lot of phonies in this business, but Dick was so genuine."

Jaworski himself is an analyst for ESPN and gives speeches when he isn't running one of his golf courses. He got his nickname, Jaws, because he was an easy interview and expressed an opinion on everything. But now, just getting to see the millionaire man from the old mills of Lackawanna, New York, takes an appointment.

SONNY JURGENSEN

In the spring of 1964, Sonny Jurgensen arrived at the Eagles' downtown office at 15th and Locust Streets to meet Joe Kuharich. Jurgensen had fully recovered from a serious arm injury suffered in a worthless postseason game called the Runner-up Bowl two years earlier. And now he was anxious to regroup under a new head coach after winning only five games in two years.

"We met for an hour or so," Jurgy said. We talked about what we were going to do. He said he wanted me to be happy and have some fun. He said we were going to win."

Then Jurgensen headed for lunch with some friends at nearby Day's Deli. A patron walked into the restaurant and spotted Jurgensen.

"Gosh, Sonny," the man said, "I see you've just been traded to the Washington Redskins."

"Get out of here," said Jurgensen. "I was just in the office."

The man was not kidding. Jurgensen, who was to become the best pure passer in the game, had been dealt to the Redskins for Norm Snead, a younger, taller quarterback with perfect manners. Kuharich believed he had traded a playboy for a Virginia preacher.

"It was April Fool's Day, but this was no joke," said Jurgensen. "I was shocked. I could not believe it. I still don't know why the trade was made."

In a perfect world, the Eagles would have followed their 1960 championship with another title. Jurgensen would have replaced Norm Van Brocklin, and the offense, with Jurgensen throwing 32 touchdown passes in 1961, would have dominated the rest of the league. But Joe Kuharich's world was far from perfect. There was an outbreak of injuries, mostly to Jurgensen's receivers. The '60 Eagles had been thin. The backups faltered in the ensuing years and Kuharich began cleaning house, shipping Jurgensen, halfback Timmy Brown, wideout Tommy McDonald, fullback Ted Dean, and

The Eagles traded Sonny Jurgensen to the Washington Redskins in 1964, after which Jurgensen tormented his former mates en route to the Hall of Fame.

cornerback Irv Cross. Jurgensen would torment the Eagles for the next 11 years and end up in the Pro Football Hall of Fame. Snead played seven years in Philadelphia, throwing 111 touchdown passes and 124 interceptions. His defenses were dreadful.

That Jurgensen got to play 18 years as a pro quarterback is remarkable. "I only threw the ball 53 times in my senior year at Duke," he said. "We had no flankers. We ran out of a full backfield. All I did was throw on occasions. That's why I've always said that playing behind Van Brocklin was a learning experience."

Charley Gauer, an Eagles assistant with a smart offensive mind, scouted Jurgensen and bought back a glowing report. "He put me through a lot of drills," said Jurgensen. "They were foreign to me. But gosh, I look back on it and these are the same drills I use today working with young boys. Gauer was great."

Later in Jurgensen's career, the Eagles were preparing to play the New York Giants. The Sam Huff—Andy Robustelli—Jim Katcavage—Dick Modzelewski Giants. Gauer wasn't coaching that year. But he and Jurgensen often watched game films together. Jurgensen asked about strategy. Gauer suggested throwing short on first downs in order to stay out of third-down trouble.

"I threw 57 times in that game," said Jurgy, "I just followed what Gauer said. "[Head coach Nick Skorich] found out about it and he was pissed."

When Jurgensen was a Redskin, coach George Allen brought his team to Albright College to scrimmage the Eagles. I was sitting alongside Rick Arrington, an injured third-string quarterback, as we watched Jurgensen throw those long, arching passes in the warmups. Jurgy threw with a kind of sidearm motion, twisting his hip into the delivery.

"Look," blurted Arrington, "the ball is a perfect spiral every time. It never wobbles."

Sonny Jurgensen's passes almost always spiraled that way. He threw 4,262 of them, completing 2,433 for 32,224 yards. He was so good at what he did that you swear he could climb out of bed and toss a ball through a moving tire 40 yards away. With a perfect spiral, of course.

DONOVAN McNABB

From a distance, Donovan McNabb appears to be a linebacker. He stands 6-foot-3 and weighs 226 pounds, not much different in size than his new teammate, linebacker Shawn Barber. His legs are thicker than the legs of some of his 300-pound linemen. But when McNabb steps into his drills, the illusion is gone. There is no doubt that you are seeing a remarkable quarterback, a natural athlete who makes throwing and running seem so easy, so right.

"He's a four-tool quarterback," says tight end Chad Lewis, in a line that appears in every McNabb feature. "He's a threat with his arm, his legs, his brains, and his heart."

In long-ago years, Donovan McNabb would have been a single-wing tailback, running those sweeps, throwing those little turn-outs and working those spin fakes with his fullback. But now, after seven seasons and 88 starts, he is poised to break most of the Eagles passing records. And as the Eagles move closer to a Super Bowl, McNabb will be under enormous pressure to win with his arm, his legs, his brains, and his heart.

"It comes with the position," he says when asked about handling the pressure of the game. "Playing the quarterback position entails a lot. It entails you being a team leader. It entails you to be prepared for everything that you definitely will be faced with. And also making sure all the guys are thinking on the right page."

In 2001, McNabb's third season, he was involved in 614 plays, or 63 percent of the Eagles' total of 974 plays. He totaled 3,715 pass-and-scramble yards, or 75.4 percent of the offensive yards. It was an unheard-of load to carry for a 25-year-old quarterback who was running a veer-option offense at Syracuse just three years earlier.

"I enjoy the challenge," McNabb said. "That's why I think a lot of us play football. We enjoy coming in and hearing people say what we can't do. They say we don't have enough firepower to compete with all the other guys. When we hear that, it just brings a smile to our faces."

Ah, that Donovan McNabb smile, so joker-like. Andy Reid, the head coach, likens his quarterback to a member of Bill Cosby's television family, suggesting fun and adventure. "That's just something that's a part of me," said McNabb. "With this team, all of us are very loose. When one guy starts, everyone else follows."

Just don't expect McNabb to smile if you call him a running quarterback. "I'm a drop-back quarterback," he said. "I'm a drop-back quarterback who, if things aren't there, I'm able to make things happen with my legs. When people begin to say I'm a running quarterback, I think they're looking at the end result instead of the whole picture of me dropping back, going through my reads and then making a decision."

The term running quarterback, of course, has been applied to black quarterbacks before. The implication was that they couldn't read defenses, so they took off. White quarterbacks, on the other hand, were regarded as clever and tricky when they scrambled.

"They call him the Michael Jordan of that team," New York Giants linebacker Michael Barrow once said.

"The films don't lie. He's a guy who just wills his team to victory. He's the heartbeat," said Seattle free safety Marcus Robertson.

On April 17, 1999, Donovan McNabb wasn't even regarded as the right choice by some fans, including Ed Rendell, the city's sports-minded mayor. WIP, the sports radio station, sent an army of fans to the draft in New York City with marching orders to support halfback Ricky Williams, the Heisman Trophy winner. When the Eagles selected McNabb with the second pick and Williams dropped to the New Orleans Saints three spots lower, the fans jeered. McNabb merely smiled, knowing those were the same fans who probably had trouble throwing a quarter into a bridge toll hopper.

The boos have turned to rocketing cheers now, as if Donovan McNabb is royalty. His soaring popularity has forced him to change addresses. "I love the kids and I love to interact with them," he said. They would show up at all hours, wanting to shoot baskets and jive talk. The crowds became too much of a distraction for McNabb, the team's hardest worker. "I just liked talking to them and providing a little guidance," McNabb said. "I decided to move because I saw a better neighborhood. Not to say the neighborhood I was living in was bad. But I just saw a place were I could have a little more privacy."

McNabb lived across the Delaware River in Cherry Hill, New Jersey. Then he became a superstar on his way to becoming an idol. Suddenly, the public relations office began acting like so many CIA agents. One PR assistant, Rich Burg, now handles all of McNabb's interviews. Ask where McNabb lives, and the line is purposely vague. "In southern New Jersey," the Eagles say. McNabb is even more evasive. "I still live in Jersey," he says.

On a slow news day last spring, the city tabloid revealed that he had become engaged to his college sweetheart, Raquel Nurse. McNabb objected to the story, which was headlined "McNabbed," and the front-page photo.

Modesty aside, McNabb laughs and works outrageous hours and tries to live an ordinary life. He doesn't wear gold chains or earrings and will never

Donovan McNabb was not a popular choice as the Eagles first round pick in 1999, but he made six Pro Bowls in eleven seasons in Philadelphia and led the team to the NFC Championship in 2004.

be caught breaking the speed limit on some interstate at 2 a.m. He simply acts ordinary and plays out of the ordinary—the ultimate joker.

There were few laughs during the 2005 season, the worst in Donovan McNabb's pro career. His passing stats dropped alarmingly, 31 TD passes to 16; 3,875 yards to 2,507. Despite a sports hernia, he made nine starts before heading to the bench when he reaggravated the injury in mid-November.

Yet, what hurt McNabb even more was a steady attack from teammate Terrell Owens, who had a love affair with the ESPN television cameras. Owens began firing verbal blasts at his quarterback soon after their Super Bowl loss. McNabb threw only one back. "Keep my name out of your mouth," he snapped and let it go at that.

The Eagles ultimately booted Owens off the team and then out of town, showing him the highway to Dallas. McNabb, of course, was joyful. "I like everybody," he said. "I love everybody. I'm a loving guy."

So McNabb was back in good humor and, seemingly, in good health. And the Super Bowl was still out there somewhere, just farther away than it was a few years ago.

TROY VINCENT

Ten years have slipped past since the Miami Dolphins picked Troy Vincent to join their dream secondary of J.B. Brown at the right corner, Jarvis Williams at strong safety and Louis Oliver at free safety. Five years later, under the free agency/salary cap system, the dream was shattered by big money. Williams went to the New York Giants, Oliver to Cincinnati, Brown to Pittsburgh, and Vincent to the Eagles.

In 1996, the year he became an Eagle, Vincent joined Bobby Taylor, the other corner, and free safety Brian Dawkins. Damon Moore, the strong safety, would follow in the 1999 draft. The old man of Andy Reid's youthful, blitz-minded defense has started 145 games. He has seen them all. Sidearmers, little 5-foot-11 scramblers, rocket-armed pocket guys, and jittery rookies.

"There's been quite a few good ones," said Vincent. "Let's start with Dan Marino. Let's start with John Elway. Then Jim Kelly and Troy Aikman." Vincent loves to play mind games with the passers, duping them into thinking they're seeing one defense when the Eagles are really into something else. "When you start talking about the Elways, the Marinos, the Kellys and the Aikmans, there are only so many mind games you can play," he said.

"They're smart. They know what to expect. They generally know what coverage you're in. The best way to play against a quarterback like that is to just line up and play and may the best man win on that particular play."

But on those Sundays when a young backup, or a rookie right off the college campus, is starting, Vincent can get inside his head. "Oh, you can move around," he said. "You can show him different looks. Those quarterbacks have not yet seen a bunch of blitzes. For example, in our scheme, we do a lot of blitzing. A lot of times there's a lot of movement, so he tries to figure out where the blitz is coming from. At the same time, I'm showing him one look. I may appear to be inside, but eventually I want to get outside. Or I may be outside, but I really want to be inside. I may be lining off, but before they snap the ball, I'm going to be at the line of scrimmage."

Vincent has faced all kinds of receivers, too. The little speed guys. The rangy leapers. The precision route runners who play their own mind games. "You know who I struggled with early in my career?" he said. "Andre Rison. Andre Rison was tough. And Andre Reed of the Bills. Andre [Rison] was a real quick guy. And you know, tough. In and out of a break real well. A real skilled athlete. He played mind games with you...tried to trick you. Andre [Reed] was a guy who had a great quarterback [Jim Kelly] in a great system. The K-Gun, that was loaded. They ran the ball well, so that made it tougher to stop."

Vincent named some others. Willie Gault, the sprinter, Flipper Anderson, the deep threat. Then he named Henry Ellard and began talking at length. "The best route runner I have ever seen," Vincent said. "When he was with the Rams, then over to Washington, he was real clever. He made everything look alike. You didn't know whether he was running a two-yard route or a 'go.' You didn't know if he was going to break off at 15 [yards] or if he was curling at eight. Everything looked the same."

Unlike many pro athletes, Vincent has looked down the road and prepared for the time when he won't be driving on receivers, wondering where the break is taking them. "I always knew I couldn't play football for life," he said. "I knew there was life after this job. And that's how I've treated it from day one. It is a job, not a career."

In his second year, Vincent bought a dog kennel in Hollywood, Florida. "I came back home and did a community bookstore," he said. Then it was land development and construction, professional services, drag racing, and investment advice.

"I've been going into different ventures," he said. "I like to consider myself an entrepreneur. I've had my peaks and valleys [he reportedly lost $40,000 on his bookstore]. But now I think I've found the right niche."

Vincent can play perhaps two more seasons. Then the pads and cleats will be hung up. Troy Vincent will come to work in stylish business suits, with colorful ties, grasping a briefcase. He will still be at the top of his game.

3

THE PLAYERS

VINCE PAPALE

Vince Papale was always counting heads. It was a little numbers game he played in his mind during the training camp warmups. In the summer of 1976, the year that Dick Vermeil arrived to coach the Eagles, Papale was a 30-year-old rookie receiver. He had learned his trade with the Philadelphia Bell, an adventurous minor-league team of NFL castoffs and small-college dreamers. His early love for track had taken him to St. Joseph's, a local college without a football program.

So each week, Papale kept counting. "When Dick made the final cut from 50 to 45, I knew I was up against it," he said. "I was never really told that I had made the team. So when we got out on the field and I was counting around, I figured if I was going to be on the roster, I'd be the 45th guy."

Suddenly, Vermeil appeared. Crouching in front of Papale as the Eagles went through their knee bends, the coach announced his decision. "Congratulations, old man," he said, "you're a Philadelphia Eagle."

"C-c-c-c-oach," Papale stammered, "can I be excused for five minutes? I've got to make a phone call."

"What's the deal?" Vermeil asked. "Who are you calling, *Sports Illustrated*, CBS and all those people?"

"No, Coach," Papale replied. "I just want to call my dad and all the guys at Westinghouse," Papale said, tears appearing in his eyes. "Can I go call the foreman at Westinghouse down here in Essington where my dad works?"

Frank "Kingie" Papale had been operating a burner for a lifetime at Westinghouse, working with large acetylene torches. "He'd burn those big pieces for the turbines in the original submarines," said Papale. "I called the foreman and said, 'Tell Kingie that his son's a Philadelphia Eagle,' I heard him yell it out, and that whole wing, the E wing at Westinghouse, just exploded. My dad got on the phone. He was crying. I was crying, too. We partied for 48 hours."

Vince Papale caught one pass in three seasons with the Eagles. His real role was covering kickoffs and punts, flying downfield and dodging elbows, forearms, and everything else. "I signed for $21,000 and got a $2,000 roster bonus," he said. "Before that, I was teaching accounting, business law, and consumer economics at my alma mater, Interboro High School. The roster bonus was the most money I had ever held in my hands at one time, and I was 30 years old."

Papale became a living Rocky. He had a rugged, handsome face that appeared carved and a free-spirited personality. The sight of Papale running with those long track strides thrilled the fans and made him an instant hero. A king, actually, in South Philadelphia, with its large Italian population.

"I loved hitting people," said Papale. "I made a lot of noise. And I knew I had to keep my head on a swivel, hoping I wouldn't get taken out. A lot of guys would take you out because I was taking them out. Jeez, you always had to watch out. They could take you out at your knees back then."

In reflecting on his brief, memorable career as an Eagle, Papale hasn't forgotten the men who prepared him for his big chance. Ron Holliday, a little 5-foot-9 receiver, taught him about how to run clean, hard routes when they were with the Philadelphia Bell. Marvin Frazier, who played briefly with the Denver Broncos, was his hands guy. Joe Gardi, a Bell coach, stayed after practice to help Papale polish his moves. "Gardi told me, 'You know, you're a great athlete, you've got a lot of heart,'" Papale recalled. "'But as a wide receiver, you suck.'" Later, there was Carmichael. He also helped Papale spend that $2,000 roster bonus at Boyd's, a popular men's clothing store.

The long shots like Vince Papale all have their dreams. Most of them end before they have a chance to unfold. This one didn't. In Philadelphia, Papale is still regarded by fans as something of a cult hero. And when some Eagles cover guy strays from his lane and overruns a tackle, they share the same thought as the burners at the Westinghouse plant. Papale would have buried the guy.

The improbable football career of Vince Papale took another crazy turn in the summer of 2006 when Walt Disney brought it to the big screen.

The Rocky-style movie, *Invincible*, featured Mark Wahlberg as Papale; Greg Kinnear as coach Dick Vermeil; and Michael Nouri as owner Leonard Tose.

CLAUDE HUMPHREY

Claude Humphrey was past his prime as a power rusher when he came out of semi-retirement to join the Eagles in 1979. But he was back with Marion Campbell, the man known as Swamp Fox, who had coached him during his big sack years in Atlanta.

The Eagles played a 3-4 scheme. The Falcons were also a 3-4 team. But they wanted Humphrey to play over the tight end, thereby minimizing his pass-rushing role. "He was like a pitcher for 13 years who is suddenly asked to play third base," said Campbell, after Humphrey retired four games into the 1978 season.

In the Eagles' rushline, Humphrey and Carl Hairston were outside with Charlie Johnson inside at the nose tackle. "I think this is the best defensive line I ever played on," Humphrey used to say. "And that's going all the way back to the beginning." Johnson had been a military policeman in Vietnam. Hairston had driven a furniture truck before being recruited for college in a pool hall. Both were seventh-round draft picks. But Humphrey was the real steal. The Eagles got him for two fourth-rounders and watched him terrorize quarterbacks on legs that seemed a lot younger than 35 years. Or was it 32 years? The Eagles' 1979 press guide lists Humphrey's birthdate as November 19, 1947. But the official NFL encyclopedia lists June 29, 1944.

Chuck Clausen was Humphrey's position coach. "The pass rusher runs with his body laid out in front of him," said Clausen. "Claude Humphrey had the perfect body lean of a pass rusher. You can always accelerate from a lean-out position. So the good pass rushers have great speed, acceleration, and a pass-rusher's body lean."

Humphrey played at Tennessee State, where winning the coin flip usually meant the defensive unit would take the field to start the game. Jeff Merrow, once Humphrey's understudy in Atlanta, was amused at Humphrey's changing ages. "Hell, he was 26 when he got out of college," said Merrow, relishing the old Humphrey stories, real or imagined. "He played there for five years. Claude was always talking about guys at Tennessee State wearing other people's jerseys. When a guy was a freshman or sophomore, and they wanted him to play another year, he'd wear someone else's jersey. Hell, Claude said he played wearing somebody else's jersey one year and the guy got drafted in the second round."

It was a pass rusher's era when Humphrey joined the Falcons in 1968. Whatever his age, Humphrey threw a wicked head slap and used his bag of moves off that initial blow. "Then they took the head slap away, and I'd say, shoot, it cost me seven sacks a year," he said. "Just off that, there were so many things I could do. But the tackle, all he had to do was sit in the hole and play my body. Then jam us in the face."

Claude Humphrey played his final three years in Philadelphia and then headed for his sprawling farm outside of Memphis, Tennessee. The one play that haunts him occurred in Super Bowl XV. Oakland's Jim Plunkett began scrambling to his side. But Humphrey was held and nearly taken down on the play. There was no flag, and Plunkett whirled and threw a sideliner to halfback Kenny King, who scored on an 80-yard play. It was virtually a knockout punch that opened a 14-0 Raider lead. In that moment, Humphrey would have needed his old head slap to reach Plunkett.

Even though he walked away from the Falcons, they didn't forget Claude Humphrey in Atlanta. When their sack total dropped to 26 in 1986, they put in a call to the farm and brought Humphrey back as a pass-rushing coach.

TIM ROSSOVICH

Prime Time? The Boz? Bad Moon? Sure, Deion Sanders, Brian Bosworth, and Andre Rison were crazy at times, playing to the television cameras as if they were actors, which they really were when the lights came on. It's likely that none of them, indeed none of today's players, ever heard of Tim Rossovich, the NFL's all-time fun-lover.

Rossovich, a fine linebacker and No. 1 draft pick, played on some dreadful Eagles teams from 1968-71. He walked off a winner only 15 times in 56 games, or about once a month. Yet Rosso never got down on himself. To the contrary, he elevated his off-field game to outrageous heights. Asked to pose for the cover of a national magazine, he doused his shaggy hair and game jersey with lighter fluid and set himself on fire.

"Some of my frat brothers were burning another guy's car one day," he once recalled. "I leaped through the flames and discovered it wasn't that big a deal to be put on fire. I guess I set myself on fire four or five times."

General manager Pete Retzlaff, a great Eagles tight end who grew up in conservative North Dakota, sensed it was all an act at the time. "It's a gimmick world," Retzlaff used to say. "People come into professional athletics with a gimmick and find themselves with more notoriety than some of the great performers."

Retzlaff didn't draft Rossovich. He was the hand-picked choice of coach-general manager Joe Kuharich, who was something of an odd thinker himself. The Eagles had allowed 409 points the year before, and Rosso was a 6-foot-4 hitter on Southern California's national championship team. Soon after arriving for his first training camp, Rossovich reflected on his strange lifestyle. "I do consider the way I live to be interesting," he said. "I think other people deserve a chance to see what I do."

Chuck Bednarik, the greatest linebacker in Eagle history, marveled at Rossovich's hard-knocks style. But he disapproved of his floppy hair. "I hate that kind of hair," Bednarik once said. "Hair like that belongs to people who carry guitars, or are in show business, or maybe laying around the beaches in California, or Atlantic City. The rest of it, he's a superman."

Rossovich had the same feeling about himself, as if his was a painless life and he was free to try anything. Just before his freshman year at USC, Rossovich engaged in a daring rope-swinging competition over the Russian River in northern California. "The object was to swing out and see who could drop closest to a pile of rocks," he said. "We did it for money. One time there was a lot of money in the pot, and I dropped too close and tore my elbow up." Two weeks later, Rosso executed a back flip into a fish pond near his frat house. His elbow became infected by the stagnant water, and Rossovich ended up in the school health center.

"I went into a coma for four days," he said. "My left arm ballooned up and I flipped out. I went into fits and convulsions and beat up some of the hospital attendants. It took six campus policemen and a straitjacket to subdue me." Later, asked to explain his wild lifestyle, he shrugged and said, "A good experience is worth anything."

Rossovich had a Pro Bowl season in 1969. But his real enjoyment came away from the field. Engaged in a discussion of insects with several friends, he suddenly saw a spider and ate it. At training camp, he began to read a letter but abruptly jumped up and started screaming, "Sexual distraction!

Sexual distraction!" He took a quick glance around the room and then was gone. That same year, he entered the training room and promptly dove head-first into a whirlpool bath. Said fullback Tom Woodeshick, another free spirit: "He must have a unique body."

There was also a serene side to Tim Rossovich. He sometimes donned a tie-dyed cape, with a monk's cowl covering his head, and black leotards. Dressed in what he called his Renaissance outfit, he would perform pirouettes and then listen to a recording of Gregorian chants.

Rossovich stopped his capers only once. As a rookie, he had a two-by-four-inch lump removed from the left side of his chest. The tumor turned out to be benign. "Before I was operated on, they said it might be malignant," he said. "I was concerned. But I didn't worry about it. Soon as I woke up, I staggered out of the hospital and fell down a few times. I didn't lose any sleep. I figured when I'm going to die, I'm going to die. It might even be fun, who knows?"

KENNY PAYNE

Everywhere he went, Kenny Payne kept them laughing. He came down from Green Bay as a free agent soon after the start of the 1977 season when the Packers grew tired of his comedy act.

Payne spent his first year on injured reserve after undergoing an emergency appendectomy. Then Payne's follies began. He started spiking the ball in practice, infuriating coach Dick Vermeil. Afterwards, Payne bragged about his receiving skills (he once caught 12 passes in a game for the Packers) and fondly called his coach "that little midget."

In the 1978 opener, Payne caught a touchdown pass from Ron Jaworski. A female reporter from the *Washington Post*, seeking an angle to next week's Redskins-Eagles game, approached Payne in the crowded dressing room. He was standing naked, facing his locker with a towel in his hand.

"Kenny," said a teammate, tapping Payne on the shoulder, "there's a girl reporter here who wants to talk to you."

Kenny Payne grinned a toothless grin. "Tell her to wait until I put my teef in," he said.

Payne played one season for the Eagles and then was released by Vermeil. He attended a season-ending party at Bookbinder's, a popular seafood restaurant. He was last seen walking out with a decorative palm tree.

FRED HILL

Joe Kuharich, the head coach of the Eagles during the turbulent mid-'60s, once said that Fred Hill had the softest hands of any receiver he ever coached. Kuharich was a master of malapropism, but this was a straight-arrow line. Hill, the Eagles' fourth-round draft pick in 1965, was an All-America receiver at Southern Cal. He had beach-boy good looks framed by blonde, wavy hair. He had enough speed to have been offered a contract as an outfielder by the Boston Red Sox and those soft hands that seemed to caress a spiraling football.

Hill caught only 85 passes in seven years for a struggling team that lived by the pass. Yet when he reflects on his career, Fred Hill thinks more about Kimberly Hill, his bouncy, ever-smiling young daughter, who developed acute lymphatic leukemia. He thinks more about Dr. Audrey Evans, the director of oncology at Children's Hospital. And he thinks about Stan Lane, a neighbor with whom he helped originate a charity called "Eagles Fly for Leukemia."

In the summer of 1969, Hill was returning from a preseason game in Raleigh, North Carolina. Hobbling to his South Jersey apartment with a cast on his injured knee, he was met by his wife, Fran, who broke the stunning news. "Soon as I found out, I could not have cared less about football," he said. "My family doctor told me Kimmy was going to die, that there was less than a one-percent chance of her making it. He gave her two years." Kim Hill was three years old.

Hill continued to play. But there were terrible distractions. Kim Hill needed to be taken to Children's Hospital every day for a week, every other week. She received chemotherapy and later radiation treatments to the brain. "It was hard when she was getting all the treatments," said Hill. "I wouldn't tell her she was receiving a spinal [tap] until we hit the [Walt Whitman] bridge. Then she would cry all the way to the hospital. We were told she could die any time."

Meanwhile, the Eagles had converted Hill into a 226-pound tight end. He moved ahead of Mike Ditka as the starter in 1968 and caught 30 passes. But then he tore a knee ligament and later tore an adductor muscle. Suddenly his career became secondary to the survival of his little daughter. "Once I hurt my knee," he said, "I never did anything. I was just around."

The Eagles began switching his position. Hill played flanker and tight end one week, then split end and tight end the next. He cut his weight to 208, often skipping lunch, to survive the shuffle. Whatever the position, Hill was consumed by what was happening to Kim Hill. There were four years of chemo and radiation and those painful spinal taps. Eventually, she entered remission, a victory that could only be described as a miracle.

In 1977, there was a prime-time movie called *Something for Joey*, the sad story of Joey Cappelletti's losing battle with leukemia. Joey was the son of John Cappelletti, the pro football running back. Fred Hill understood the medical odds, but he couldn't bring himself to watch the terrible ending to Joey Cappelletti's life.

At the time, Kim Hill was attending Mission Viejo elementary school in southern California. She was on the swimming team. Her father, now out of football, had become the owner of McDonald's franchises in Mission Viejo and later Rancho Santa Marguerita. Then Kim suffered a near-tragic relapse. Doctors removed a softball-sized tumor near her brain after she had experienced numbness in one of her arms. She has undergone three additional operations in the past seven years. The most recent surgery was performed in January, 2002, after a 911 call.

"It was bad," said Fred Hill. "It took eight hours and involved the sagital side of the brain that determines right and left [commands]. They took out 80 percent of the tumor. And now she's more alert and she's added strength." Kim can also talk, move her right arm, and sit up, simple tasks that are considered remarkable by the Hill family.

Kim Hill is now confined to a wheelchair and lives in a nursing facility not far from San Juan Capistrano, where the Hills live. Fred Hill seldom thinks about his pro football career, except when he meets one of his old teammates, like Jim Skaggs, a pulling guard, or Ollie Matson, who finished his legendary career with the Eagles.

"To be honest, I've always felt like a total failure," said Hill. "I had such big plans and hopes. But it's funny. The Eagles were going to play me on defense at one time. I practiced at tight safety with the college All-Stars and once tackled Gale Sayers."

Hill's career lends itself to the big second-guess. According to John McKay, his college coach, Hill could have signed a $100,000 contract with the New York Jets. McKay told Hill it was one of those American Football League deals made by Oakland owner Al Davis during a secret draft in the premerger war years. He also had a baseball offer from the Red Sox and might have played alongside Carl Yastrzemski if his ailing back had held up.

As a receiver, Fred Hill never lived up to his lofty expectations. But he is most proud of his success as a father. Fred's daughter Kim is living with leukemia.

"But we loved Philadelphia," said Hill. "All the new experiences. We came from a poor family and we had never been to Washington or New York. Every trip was like excitement to us." He paused. "I guess I did all right," Fred Hill said.

TOM WOODESHICK

Even today, 38 years later, Tom Woodeshick can still remember breaking into the open on a trap play against the Chicago Bears. There was a gaping hole, mostly created by massive right tackle Bob Brown, and Woodeshick took it. Took it 60 yards into the end zone on the final play of the first half. Unfortunately, the touchdown was nullified by an illegal procedure call against left tackle Lane Howell, blocking on the backside, maybe 10 yards from Woody's breakaway.

The Eagles finished with a 2-12 record that year. So why does Woodeshick remember how one tackle gave him a touchdown and the other took it away? That was his finest year as a power back. He finished with 947 yards, third highest total in the league. But runners are measured by 1,000-yard seasons, and that 60-yard trap play cost Woodeshick a chance to join the big club.

"I had a 4.4-yard aveuage that year," Woodeshick said. "We really ran the ball a lot in '68, and I got close to 1,000. But it doesn't take a mathematician to figure out if you run 300 times and average 4.4 yards, you get your 1,000. The most I ever ran was 217 times. And we played only 14 games until 1978, when they went to 16, two more games."

Woodeshick also remembers getting knocked out of a game against Minnesota the same year. Earlier that season, he was also ejected from a game against Dallas, a team he personally despised. Woodeshick objected to a late hit by Phil Clark on a kickoff return. Woody sprinted off the bench. Soon he and safety Mike Gaechter were exchanging words and punches. "I nailed them both, Clark and Gaechter," said Woodeshick. Gaechter was also tossed. "It was like trading a pig for a pork chop," piped Eagle linebacker Dave Lloyd. With Woodeshick gone, the Cowboys easily won, 45-13.

Even without his 1,000-yard season, Woodeshick is remembered in Philadelphia for his sheer power, body lean, and most of all, for his will to win. "When I run, I put my guts and everything else into it," he used to say. "I'm like a man with a circulatory system speeded up five times." To work himself into shape, Woodeshick used to play his own mind game, entering the weight room wearing a pair of plastic goggles. "It gives me a sense of superiority," he would say. "I feel like some super-human from outer space. Sometimes it reminds me of the days when I was a German commando in World War One."

A funny guy, Tom Woodeshick. Even when the enemy wasn't around, he always found an opponent of sorts. At West Virginia, he used to punch out parking meters. "I loved to put a dime in them and give it my best forearm shot," he said. "It would still be on an hour for days."

Woodeshick was an eighth-round draft pick. A few Eagle scouts projected him as a strong safety. Unknown to them, he signed a $9,500 contract and got a $1,250 bonus check from the AFL's Buffalo Bills. Woodeshick signed with the Eagles, too, getting a $2,000 bonus and a $12,000 contract. His contract with the Bills, updated so he could compete in track, was later ruled invalid.

"I have some ambivalence about [coach] Joe Kuharich," he said. "Joe gave me an opportunity when I came to Philadelphia in 1963. I weighed 202 pounds playing behind Timmy Brown. There was no prospect of me getting off the bench. So I put on 28 pounds, up to 230, because I thought I had a better shot at playing fullback."

Kuharich arrived in 1964 and promptly got rid of two other fullbacks, Clarence Peaks and Ted Dean, and traded a No. 1 pick and linebacker Lee Roy Caffey for Earl Gros, a young Green Bay fullback. "I knew I was better than Gros," said Woodeshick. "Unfortunately, for four and a half years, I sat behind him. And these were the prime years of my career."

Woody missed the 1,000-yard club in 1968. The next year, he came close again with 831 yards. He missed two games, once because of the death of his mother-in-law and the other because of a broken ankle.

"That didn't hurt as much as wasting four and a half years," he said reflectively. "You know, I ran against Timmy [Brown] and ripped past him by four yards in the 40. Remember the world's fastest guy, Frank Budd? I just missed beating him at 40 yards by a pubic hair."

In Wilkes-Barre, where Woodeshick grew up, they remember him with a unique fondness. Woody was the son of a $20-a-day jury loader in the mines. "I never had a car," he said. "I never had a girl, either. Heck, I never came out of my shell until I went to college. I was an introvert."

He was an overachiever, a player who gave everything he had to give on every snap of the ball. I always called them honest players. Through high school, college and the pros, Tom Woodeshick never won a single championship. But as an individual back, and earlier as a special teams banger, he was his own champion. "Hell," he said, "I don't think I was ever booed. I loved Philly. They cheered me as a rookie, and I only carried the ball five times. It was a good marriage."

Woodeshick's real marriage was tragic. His first wife, Marsha, died in 1988 of cancer. One of his sons, Michael, died of lifelong heart disease at age 22.

DON CHUY

The medical term is polycythemia vera. It means an abnormally high count of red blood cells that can get in each other's way and form an embolism, or clot. Don Chuy, who was acquired by the Eagles in a 1969 trade with the Los Angeles Rams, learned about polycythemia vera in a sports column. Then he called his lawyer.

Any player-lawyer action in a medical case calls for some background. Chuy, a journeyman guard, and tackle Joe Carollo both came to the Eagles in that trade. They were part of a rebuilding plan under Pete Retzlaff, the new general manager, and Jerry Williams, the new head coach.

Late in his first season with the Eagles, Chuy suffered a severe contusion in his left shoulder. A month later, he developed blood-spitting and fluid in the right side of his chest, symptoms of a pulmonary embolism, or clot. Chuy was hospitalized for the final three weeks of the season. According to Dr. James Nixon, the team physician, Chuy was sidelined by a pulmonary embolism in his lung. "He was given anticoagulants, and the embolism cleared," said Dr. Nixon.

That's when Chuy's story turned into an ugly confrontation with club management. Chuy had returned to his home in North Hollywood, California, when he learned about the sports column that mentioned polycythemia vera.

"What's it all mean?" he asked Dr. John Perry, his family physician. According to Chuy, Dr. Perry described polycythemia vera as a "serious...fatal disease."

Understandably, Chuy became an angry man, blaming the Eagles for his condition and sinking into a depressed state. He lost 65 pounds in six weeks, worrying about the strange medical term and what it all meant. He even considered suicide. "I took my .38 revolver down from a closet shelf," he said in a first-person newspaper story. "I loaded the gun. I just didn't know what I wanted to do. Then my daughter started to cry. I jumped up and put the gun behind a carved wooden bear on top of the fireplace. It was my daughter's crying in her sleep that made me realize that taking a life, even your own, was God's most unforgivable sin."

Then Chuy's case took a dramatic turn. Dr. Perry told him that the diagnosis was wrong and that he wasn't suffering from polycythemia vera "or any related disease." Chuy was subsequently seen by Dr. Dick Harrell in Philadelphia, who took a lung scan and other tests. He concluded that Chuy's circulation had returned to normal. Dr. Harrell also said that Chuy's condition was actually polycythemia, which is far less serious than polycythemia vera. Dr. Harrell's final word to Chuy: don't play any more football.

"How he was ever labeled as having polycythemia vera I am sure I do not know," Dr. Harrell said. Actually, Dr. Nixon had been asked by a reporter to explain the term. In the heavy medical language and confusion that followed, the reporter jumped to the erroneous conclusion that Chuy was a victim of the more serious disease.

Anyway, Chuy filed a $1 million suit against the Eagles and collected $130,590 in back pay and damages. He took Dr. Harrell's advice and retired at 28 with his award.

LOUIE GIAMMONA

When Louie Giammona joined the Eagles as a New York Jets castoff in 1978, some of his new teammates grew suspicious. The offense already had its star back, Wilbert Montgomery, and the Eagles had drafted a kid named Ben Cowins, a star at Arkansas. Besides, Giammona was undersized at 5-foot-9, about as tall as the coach, who happened to be Dick Vermeil, Giammona's uncle.

"I was the nephew of the head coach, and I was a 5'9", 175-pound white back," said Giammona. "Everybody thought that to be able to run the ball, you had to be 6'2", 275 pounds, run the 40 in 4.2 and lift up the planet."

Giammona's duty, however, was the hammer-and-tongs variety. He turned up on all of Vermeil's special teams and made an impression. "It's not normal to run downfield as fast as you can through the blockers," he said. "So I was a little hesitant at first, sort of like walking on eggs." But then Giammona became his own psychologist. "I'd put on my helmet before the game and go out behind a hot dog stand," he said. "I'd bang my head against the wall, kind of knock myself senseless. I was on the kickoff return and kickoff coverage teams. So I knew I was going to be involved with the opening kickoff."

He was so tough and so obsessed with knocking people around that the Eagles elected Giammona to captain the special teams in 1980-82. "It was 44-1," he said. "I didn't vote for myself."

Giammona also flashed his running form in 1980, the year the Eagles reached the Super Bowl. He started six games, and the Eagles won all six. Against the Chicago Bears, he rushed 19 times for 79 yards and threw a key option pass that set up the winning field goal.

Later that season, the Eagles lost to Oakland in Super Bowl XV. Giammona partially blames his uncle for the defeat. "Obviously, we were the best team in the league," he said. "We went to Tampa on a Wednesday to practice. On Monday and Tuesday, it was cold as hell in Philadelphia. Dick was out there coaching a guy named [tight end Ken] Dunek. He was on injured reserve and wasn't going to play, and we were standing out there watching Dick coach him."

Giammona said Vermeil's Super Bowl workouts lasted three and a half hours. He roomed with John Bunting, the linebacker. "I remember saying to him on the morning of the game, 'This is the biggest day of my life and I feel like [bleep.] My back is screwed up. My knees are sore.' Dick doesn't want to hear this. But he overworked the [bleep] out of us."

BOBBY JACKSON

It is one of the ironies of the sports world. Bobby Jackson, a second-string safety, was drafted and cut in 1959 by Vince Lombardi, Green Bay's new head coach. The Eagles claimed Jackson, who made a game-saving tackle against the Packers the next year in the 1960 championship game that was Lombardi's only playoff loss.

"Prior to the game, [Tom] Brookshier had hurt his groin, and we didn't know if he was going to play," said Jackson. "I practiced a lot that week. I knew all about Boyd Dowler and Max McGee, and I was scared to death. But Tom got well and played. I was the fifth defensive back on the final series. I was playing the deep middle. But I saw what Bart [Starr] was going to do, which was throw a swing pass to Jim Taylor. I was on about the seven-yard line. Fortunately, I hit him low and kept Jim Taylor from cutting to the outside. Then Chuck [Bednarik] came in and sat on top of him. There were about seven seconds left, and then the game was over."

After being drafted and cut by Green Bay in 1959, Bobby Jackson
came back to haunt the Packers in the championship game.

According to Robert Riger, a photographer shooting from the end zone, Taylor would have scored if he had been able to elude Jackson. Yet whenever the game is replayed in the minds of old-time Eagle fans, Bednarik emerges as the hero. Bobby Jackson is regarded as the set-up guy, like a hockey winger passing off to the star scorer. Forty-two years later, Jackson shrugs off any fame that eluded him.

"Chuck and I were shown on the football cover of a book," Jackson said. "The great and the poor, they said. I was in on the tackle, but Chuck deserves all the credit. He was the greatest football player who ever lived. He was a real man. It was just an honor for me to help out on that tackle."

Jackson played only one more year. But he delivered the most famous tackle in Eagles history on the league's toughest fullback and earned a glittering championship ring. "I've got it on," said Bobby Jackson, pride ringing in his voice.

IRV CROSS

The years slip past, and so the players at MacAlester College, a Divison III school in Minnesota, remember their athletic director as a sportscaster on the set with Jimmy the Greek. But if they brushed up on their football history, they would realize that Irv Cross was also a rarity, a cornerback who could both cover and tackle.

Cross figures he suffered four concussions in 1961, his rookie year. More of those woozy collisions followed, but Cross kept banging away at receivers, giving more than he was taking. But not against the Pittsburgh Steelers.

"I had my jaw broken at old Forbes Field," said Cross. "I got kicked from behind. Then I had two or three other concussions. The next week, I had a new helmet made, with padding inside and outside. But it was all kind of dumb. I never missed a game. I used to lead with my head. I'd put my helmet into somebody's gut and blow them back. I'd tackle Jim Brown, or John David Crow, that way. I remember Erich Barnes with the 49ers. I was covering punts, and he hit me across the side of my head, cracking my jaw."

Cross watches the modern-day corners, some of whom can tackle, and winces in disgust. "It disturbs me to see the way they tackle," he said. "I don't know...I don't know. It's just a different game."

It was Cross' fate to be drafted the year after the Eagles won an NFL championship. "We thought we were good enough to win it again," said Cross. The Eagles finished 10-4 in 1961, ending up in a tainted postseason game known as the Playoff Bowl. "We were decimated by injuries," recalled Cross. "Sonny [Jurgensen] had his arm ripped out and had shoulder surgery. King Hill popped an Achilles tendon. Marion Campbell retired. [Norm] Van Brocklin had left. Pete Retzlaff played with a cast over his broken right arm."

The Eagles swooped to 3-10-1 and 2-10-2 in 1962-63, and then Joe Kuharich, who came to be known as Trader Joe, began dismantling a once-great team. Cross was sent to the Los Angeles Rams in the shakeup. He later coached the Eagles' defensive backs in 1969-70. Yet he can't shake the memories of those early '60s, when he and Tom Brookshier were working their sledgehammer ways with receivers, and Don "The Blade" Burroughs and Bobby Freeman were taking care of the deep zones.

"I was the green kid on the corner," said Cross. "I filled in for Brookie when he got hurt. Jimmy Carr was on the other corner. One of the things that helped us was our coach, Jerry Williams. He was the most innovative guy. We came up with the defense they're running today, the nickel defense. We played the Bears, and we knew we had to stop Mike Ditka. So we took a linebacker out, Pelly [Bob Pellegrini], I think, and put in a fifth back. We called it the Chicago Special, or the Ditka Special. George Allen saw it and took it to Los Angeles and called it the nickel defense."

JOHN BUNTING

He arrived in camp in 1974 driving a 1965 Volkswagen with 175,000 miles on the odometer. More specifically, John Bunting arrived at the picket line in his $100 Bug, the one with the dents on all four of the fenders.

"That was my second car," said Bunting. "I bought a 1960 Volkswagen with my $2,500 in Senior Bowl money. I got the '65 model for a hundred bucks when I got my degree at North Carolina." Bunting played outside linebacker for the Tar Heels and made a lot of tackles. But he was undersized at 205 pounds. The scouts soured on him because of his size, and the Eagles took him as a long shot on the 12th round of the 1972 draft.

"I had seven roommates that year," recalled Bunting. "The Hawk came knocking on that door six different times during training camp. I thought it would be for me, but it was always somebody else. I roomed with a lot of kickers." According to Bunting, coach Eddie Khayat put a priority on developing a team chemistry. "He wanted to introduce the rookies to a veteran team. So we had regular parties. It was scary. The veteran guys would drink shots of water and the rookies would be drinking sambuca. Eddie

John Bunting played 11 seasons for the Eagles and emerged as a union hawk. In 1982, Bunting's final year, the players held out for 57 days, almost costing the NFL its season.

loved those parties. Halfway through the season, he'd say, 'You boys still having those parties?'"

Bunting remembers a road game against the New York Giants when he was a rookie. The Giants rolled it up, routing the Eagles 62-10. "Everybody tried to run and hide in the Yankee Stadium clubhouse after the game," said Bunting. Khayat was furious. "All but my three 'Billies' quit on me," Khayat kept screaming in that distinctive Mississippi drawl. "Billy Bradley, Billy Walik, and Wild Bill Cody. They didn't quit on me. The rest of you, if your ass was on fire, I wouldn't piss on it."

Earlier that season, Khayat tried to pump up his rookies before a road game in Kansas City.

"Bunting, you ready to play?" the coach snapped.

"Sure," said Bunting. "I'm ready to go, Coach."

Khayat turned to Davis, a seldom-used back.

"Al, get used to running the ball this week," Khayat said. "Willie Lanier is going to flat-ass kill our backs."

Khayat was fired after the Eagles finished 2-11-1. But Bunting survived, playing 11 purposeful seasons for the Eagles and emerging as a union hawk. In 1982, Bunting's final year, the players held out for 57 days, almost costing the NFL its season. By then, Bunting was a fiery player rep, promising that "blood will flow in the streets" if the players' demands weren't met. He became a highly successful college coach before moving up to the Rams and Saints. Then he returned as the head coach at North Carolina, where the staff always drives shiny new cars.

JIM "GUMMY" CARR

Laughing and moving. Moving and laughing. Jim "Gummy" Carr hardly ever stopped to take life seriously, except when he was out on the field. Or just outside the lines as a secondary coach when his nomadic playing career ended in 1965.

"I started out as a running back with the Chicago Cardinals," Carr said. "You know who I played behind? Ollie Matson and Dave Mann. Then I went to cornerback. Then to strong safety. Then to linebacker. The coaches said to me, 'You've got one more move, to a down lineman.' I said, 'I'm out of here.'"

Carr played the corner on the Eagles' 1960 championship team. He was a 208-pound banger, maybe the biggest corner in the league. The Redskins, a

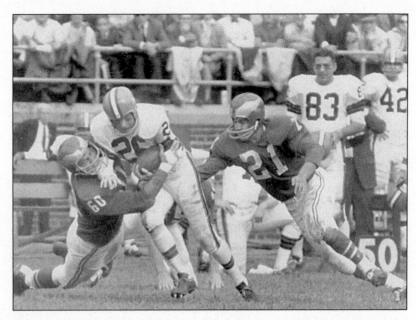

Jim "Gummy" Carr (21) closes in on Cleveland's Ray Renfro in 1961, with an assist from Chuck Bednarik (60). Carr earned his nickname in college, when he played without front teeth.

win-one, lose-one team in 1964-65, used him as a linebacker. But Carr's best years came later, when he coached secondaries in Minnesota, Chicago, Philadelphia, and Atlanta. Carr kept them loose and laughing with his jokes and tales of his adventurous nightlife.

In their 1970 camp, the Eagles worked hard on their pursuit. In a drill aimed at getting all 11 defenders flowing to the ball in their proper lanes, Carr ran with his young gladiators and promptly fell down when a strung-out sweep reached the edge of a grassy knoll.

"He was out all night," said Jerry Williams, the head coach, shaking with laughter. "The funny thing, though, is that he doesn't drink."

In truth, Williams was only exaggerating another Gummy Carr story. But not the drinking angle. Even during his playing days when the Eagles used to spend Mondays at a Chestnut Street taproom, Carr opted for 7-Up. He also never touched a weight.

"I was not very strong, that's for sure," said Carr. "I never lifted weights my whole career, college or pro. In Philadelphia, we didn't have much of a weight program. We always felt the weightlifters looked a little 'quiffy' out there lifting."

Carr's football career ended overseas as a coach with the World Football League. "When I was 61, I turned my life over to God," said Carr, who beat the Giants in a key 1960 game with a timely interception return. "Winning the championship wasn't the biggest thing; it was turning over my life to the Lord." The next year, Carr was hired to coach in Amsterdam.

"[My wife] went with me," said Carr. "I did my coaching and she went to Austria for six weeks. The hills were alive with the sound of music." Carr was laughing again; moving again.

"Let me tell you about the greatest defensive back I ever coached, Deion Sanders," said Jimmy Carr. "I taught him everything he knows. That's my claim to fame." But not Carr's only claim. "I was one of the all-time great jitterbug dancers in the league," he said. Indeed, when he was a coach, Carr introduced himself in a unique way. He would often startle a new Eagles secretary by jumping up on her desk and doing a few fast steps, his eyes ablaze with laughter. "I could pick 'em up and lay 'em down," he said.

The nickname Gummy? "I went through my whole college career without my front teeth," Carr said. "I was born and raised in the country, and I wasn't great about cleaning and brushing. Somebody came up with the nickname in my freshman year in college."

JIM McMAHON

He was 31 and his arm was shot. His knees were gimpy. But Jim McMahon still had a head for the game and a will to win. "In terms of playing with pain, he's the first guy I'd always think of," said Otho Davis, the Eagles' late trainer. "I thought I'd seen the toughest until No. 9 [McMahon] got here. Keith Krepfle was tough. Ron Jaworski was a tough old sonofagun. But they don't come down the pike any tougher than Jim McMahon."

In 1991, the Eagles were riddled with quarterback injuries. Randall Cunningham tore knee ligaments in the opener. McMahon, who would start 11 games, went down with a sprained knee in the fifth game. In came a jittery rookie free agent named Brad Goebel, who threw six interceptions and no touchdown passes in three losses. Back came McMahon, who started the next seven games despite painful knees and bruised ribs. Goebel lost another game, and Jeff Kemp mopped up in the closer.

The Eagles finished 10-6, missing a playoff on one of those crazy tie-breakers. McMahon went 8-3 as a starter, playing with pain and getting the most out of his weak elbow with the aid of massages and injections. He beat Cleveland on the road, 32-30, by throwing three scoring passes after the Eagles trailed, 23-0. McMahon, who had a cutting relationship with reporters, always said of his surprising form, "I'm throwing the ball better than I've ever thrown it," and let it go at that.

McMahon, Jimmy Mac to his teammates, played three years in Philadelphia. Three years later, he was warming up as a Green Bay backup to Brett Favre. Seeing the soft wobblers and the knee braces that bulged under McMahon's gold-colored game pants, an official playfully suggested that he should retire. McMahon, who was then 37, took his advice.

WILLIE RAINES

In the summer of 1974, Willie Raines lugged the heaviest boom box any of the Eagles had ever seen around the Widener University campus. Raines never attended college. But in the '70s, teams frequently brought up to 100 prospects into training camp. Raines was a 6-foot-2, 288-pound offensive tackle who had played with the Golden Barracudas, a semipro team in Florida. "I do what a Funkman do," explained Raines, his head tilted towards the boom box. When the players struck that summer, Willie Raines actually played in a preseason game. He kept it loose until the strikers came off the picket lines, and he rejoined the Barracudas.

KEVIN ALLEN

Old scouts remember the 1985 draft as the year of the pass protectors. There were six offensive linemen taken on the first round alone. Bill Fralic...Lomas Brown...Ken Ruettgers...Jim Lachey...Trevor Matich...and the one the Eagles would rather forget, Kevin Allen.

Allen, a 285-pound tackle from Indiana, signed a $1.65-million contract and earned 42 glowing lines in the team's press guide. Coach Marion Campbell even raved about his character, noting that Allen played under three different coaches at Indiana and "progressed each season." The Eagles waved him into the lineup as a confused rookie starter. So Kevin Allen began believing what his ego told him, that he was destined to become a great pro player.

Allen was benched after giving up eight and a half sacks in the first four games. His career then blew up. Allen was released on September 30, 1986, after he was charged with raping a woman and beating her male companion at 5:30 a.m. in a Labor Day assault in Margate, New Jersey, a beachfront community. He is now regarded as the biggest draft bust in Eagles history.

HERM EDWARDS

The odds of Herm Edwards scoring on his bizarre fumble return against the New York Giants in 1978 were once in a lifetime. Edwards, a cornerback with ordinary speed but extraordinary instincts, was probably on the field for more than 9,000 plays in his career. But that touchdown return, all on pure instincts in a game in which a quarterback kneel was all the Giants needed to win, defined Edwards' nine-year career with the Eagles.

The Giants led the Eagles 17-12 with 31 seconds to play. With the Eagles out of timeouts, every Giant knew that the final play would be a well-rehearsed kneel-down by Joe Pisarcik, the quarterback.

"A couple of plays before that, they had run the ball," recalled Edwards, now the head coach of the New York Jets. "The next play they tried to fall down. Bill [Bergey] and [Frank] LeMaster kind of knocked [center] Jim Clack into Pisarcik, and there was a little skid. So there was some indecision there on the final play. I'm on the backside, talking to [Doug] Kotar. He thought they were going to fall on the ball." So did Herm Edwards.

"Yeah, congratulations," Edwards said to Kotar. "We'll see you again at the end of the season."

Pisarcik, who joined the Eagles the next season, filled Edwards in with the other crazy details when he arrived. "Joe said he was going to hand it off to [Larry] Csonka," said Edwards. "But the ball got snapped in a little bit of a hurry. There was so much indecision involved. He said when Clack got up to the line, he looked up at the clock and didn't want the time to expire. So he snapped the ball and Joe bobbled it. The timing was off. It went off Csonka's hip. I saw all of this happening, and I kind of got Kotar and jerked him out of the way. The ball took a bounce and I tore right in and got it. My instincts were to catch it and run. You know, the coaches always tell you to fall on it, but the clock would have run out."

Edwards, toting the bouncing ball, ran 26 yards into the end zone, ahead of his shrieking teammates. The play, which gave the Eagles a shocking 19-17 win, became known as the Miracle of the Meadowlands. "It was all quiet at that point," said Edwards. "Except on our side, where we were all celebrating."

Two years later, Herm Edwards wasn't as lucky. It was early in Super Bowl XV, and the Oakland Raiders held a 7-0 lead. Jim Plunkett began scrambling when pressured by the Eagle pass rush. "We were in a cover-two deep, with a five-underneath shell," said Edwards, the right corner. "Cliff Branch ran up the rail and Kenny King swung into the flat."

In Edwards' mind, the coverage was perfect. Seeing Plunkett in trouble, Edwards sensed he had to move up and keep Plunkett from scrambling to a first down. "Branch took [safety] Brenard Wilson out of the play," Edwards said. "I didn't have anybody behind me." Plunkett, now desperate, lofted a little sideline pass, just out of Edwards' reach. But it was perfect for King, who flew 80 yards down the left sideline for the touchdown that doomed the Eagles. "It nicked my fingernails," said Edwards.

Herm Edwards, the son of an army sergeant, signed as a free agent for a $10,000 bonus. He played the right corner for nine years in Philadelphia. "I think they appreciated someone like me," he said. "I was a blue-collar guy. I could have signed with Miami, but this was an excellent opportunity to have a fresh start. I told myself, 'I'm going to Philly.'"

After his playing career ended in 1985, Edwards remained in the game as a coach. In 2001, he became the first African-American head coach in the New York Jets' 42-year history. "I have to believe this was his destiny," said Dick Vermeil, Edwards' coach with the Eagles. "It's his time; he's paid his dues."

Five years later, following a tough 4-12 season marked by quarterback injuries and weak defense, Edwards moved on to Kansas City, where he succeeded Vermeil.

"Guys sometimes come into this league and think it's a right," said Edwards. "But it's not a right; it's a privilege to play in the National Football League. It's a privilege to coach. Privilege is when you go to practice, or you go to work, and you try to become the best player, or the best coach you can possibly be that day. Because you owe it. You owe it to football."

LEROY KEYES

Once, just before the Eagles started another training camp day, I asked Leroy Keyes how far he could throw a football. At Purdue, where he had been a great running back and safety, Keyes had thrown "some little dinky option passes." But on this summer morning, he unleashed a pass that sailed 78 yards.

"That's when I was young and the arm was strong," laughed Leroy Keyes, probably the greatest all-around athlete ever drafted by the Eagles. At Purdue, Keyes ran, caught, returned kicks and threw those little fake-sweep passes. When there was an opposing star receiver to cover, he played superb pass defense. He was runner-up to O.J. Simpson for the Heisman Trophy and the second player drafted behind Simpson in 1969.

At the end of his rookie season, Keyes suffered a terrible injury from which he never fully recovered. The Eagles were practicing at Stanford in Palo Alto, California, for their game against the San Francisco 49ers the next day. There was a double-screen called, which sent Keyes into the right flat. "Norm [Snead] threw it to me," recalled Keyes. "I went to push off on my right foot, and his [linebacker Adrian Young] foot came on my right foot and pulled it down."

With the help of Novocaine and a generous amount of tape, Keyes played against the 49ers, carrying the ball 10 times before being pulled for Cyril Pinder, his backup. He then was told not to engage in any activity for the next six weeks.

"I was at Temple one day, McGonigle Hall, and some kids were shooting baskets," he said. "I'd take the ball and bounce it back to them. I reached up as the ball was coming through the net and felt a pop that sounded like a shot from somewhere. I had no motion in my right foot."

They operated on Leroy Keyes the next day to repair a torn Achilles tendon. Over the next three seasons, there was a slight limp to Keyes' gait and what seemed to be a mile of tape wrapped around his right foot. A super spat, if you will. After his fourth year, the Eagles traded Keyes to Kansas City. He carried the ball two times and caught one pass in three games for the Chiefs, and he was finished with pro football.

"I enjoyed my four years in Philadelphia," says Keyes, who now works as an assistant director in Purdue's fundraising club. "I grew as a person. No one goes out to deliberately rupture an Achilles tendon. The medical treatment was better then than it was for Otto Graham, or Y.A. Tittle. But now, a kid blows out an ACL [anterior cruciate ligament] and he's running full-speed in three months."

Keyes can only think about what might have been if the Eagles had converted him to a strong safety. Bill Bradley, a free safety drafted the same year, became a Pro Bowler.

"The thing that hurt more than anything else was that the coach [Jerry Williams] didn't understand the players he had," said Keyes. "Pete [general manager Pete Retzlaff], I think, intimidated him. We had Cyril Pinder, Harry Jones, Harry Wilson, all those different running backs. Woody [Tom Woodeshick] was the premier fullback. We had five unhappy players trying to get two or three carries when they could."

Williams was fired early in his third year. His successor was Ed Khayat, who vowed to bring the Eagles together through a firm hand. "They treated players like it was a tinker-toy," said Keyes. "Okay, this player doesn't fit, they went to some other guy. There was a tinker-toyism approach. Somebody would play half the game and they would look at some new guy and see what he could do. I thought we had some great athletes. Bill Bradley...[Tim] Rossovich...Adrian Young...Gary Pettigrew...Mel Tom...Don Hultz. In the locker room, we just didn't jell. We got caught up in going out and studying how we looked. And with Coach Khayat, it was military. You had to be clean-shaven. The coaches were not like we wanted them to be. They were concerned about how we dressed instead of let's kick the [bleep] out of the opponent."

Keyes swung to the positives of his experience. "I got to meet some excellent people," he said. "[General manager] Jim Murray and other folks. Even [owner] Leonard Tose. He was a magnificent person to play for. It was a good journey into the night. Now we're on the other side of the night, and we're living life as best we can."

BLENDA GAY

The day was cold and gray. Ed Garvey, the executive director of the NFL Players Association, took a late-morning Metroliner from Washington, D.C., and then a cab from Philadelphia's 30th Street station across the wind-whipped Delaware River to Camden, New Jersey.

The body of Blenda Gay lay in an open casket near the altar of the Kaighn Baptist Church. There were several television crews and a few reporters and some curiosity-seekers, drawn by the remote TV trucks outside. "Except for

Blenda Gay, a 6-foot-5, 255-pound defensive end who played two seasons with the Eagles, was stabbed to death by his wife in 1976. He was 26. Roxanne Gay was found not guilty by reason of insanity in 1978.

the onlookers and the curious gawkers, there was virtually nobody there," recalled Garvey. "They were standing outside because they wanted to see a football player. How sad."

The date was December 23, 1976. Gay, a 6-foot-5, 255-pound defensive end in his second year with the Eagles, had been stabbed to death three days earlier with an eight-inch kitchen knife. He was 26.

"I came to pay my respects because he was a member of our union," said Garvey, "just as much as the executive director. What happens in a situation like that is that you want to make sure things are taken care of properly. I'll never forget taking the train back and thinking how rootless an athlete is. He can come from, say, Michigan to Philadelphia, and when the holidays come, he has no base in that community."

We drove across the Ben Franklin Bridge to the train station. Gay's murder had been the lead story in all of the papers that week. Earlier, one of the ambitious television reporters had learned Garvey's identity and proposed an interview. The shot would have used the open casket as a backdrop. Garvey winced at the idea and declined. "That was an awful day," he said. "It was a totally open casket, the whole length of his body. The whole day was bizarre."

In the days and months that followed, Roxanne Gay was charged with the predawn murder of her husband. In her defense, she recited a long history of physical abuse by Gay. In March, 1978, the 5-foot-1 mother of Gay's year-old daughter was found not guilty by reason of insanity.

Gay was buried on Christmas Day in rural Farmville, North Carolina.

ERNIE CALLOWAY

He arrived in training camp with wing-like arms that seemed to dangle to his kneecaps. Ernie Calloway, known as Spiderman to his new Eagles teammates, quickly became a presence, on and off the field.

"I'm tough," Calloway announced. "Nobody can hurt me." Spiderman lined up at defensive end for a team that had gone 2-12 the previous year. The Eagles, it seems, couldn't win for losing. At the end of the 1968 season, they upset Detroit and Minnesota, losing the right to draft O. J. Simpson.

Instead, the Eagles took Leroy Keyes, a gifted Purdue halfback, and Calloway, a towering lineman from Texas Southern, on the first two rounds. Calloway soon tangled himself in money and injury problems and was traded after his fourth season. But before he departed, Spiderman left behind a legacy of adventure and outrageous quotes.

He had mischievous eyes the size of ping-pong balls and a habit of creating problems for Pete Retzlaff, the general manager. "I haven't the slightest idea of what he's going to do next," Retzlaff used to say. In his first three years, Calloway showed promise. Yet he seemed to drift into trouble. Calloway had knee surgery, then tore a ligament when his foot caught in a trackside fence at Liberty Bell Park, where he liked to watch the horses run. He once left camp three times in one month, heading out of town in his gleaming yellow Mark III Continental. Each time, Calloway said he was quitting to work as a bricklayer in Orlando, Florida, his home town.

Calloway stood 6-foot-6, a majestic figure in pads. But he weighed only 245 pounds. In his final year as a starter, he bulked up to 280 pounds, only to flunk an electrocardiogram test. "I didn't do anything in the off-season except sleep and eat," he told reporters. "The only exercise I got was moving my television set around. It got so that I could just feel all the food just sliding down to my belly and sticking there. Maybe I should call up Dr. [Christian] Barnard. He could fix me up with a new pump. But how would it look getting my battery recharged in the huddle between plays?"

Everybody laughed at Calloway's fantasy. Those large eyes laughed, too. Eventually, Calloway was swapped to Kansas City, where he was waived out of pro football. Presumably, he headed for the nearest race track to visit the betting windows.

"I've become the greatest handicapper in the world," he once said in Philadelphia. "I'm better than the Racing Form."

JEFF BOSTIC

There were 17 centers taken in the 1980 draft. Jeff Bostic wasn't one of them. Bostic was a 240-pound snapper from Clemson, undersized but agile and with great bloodlines. His brother was Joe Bostic, a 10-year guard with the St. Louis Cardinals.

Bostic was an Eagle who got away. Signed as a free agent, Bostic survived until the final cut. I remember spotting Bostic and linebacker Mike Curcio in a fast-food restaurant near West Chester University, having their last training camp meal with grim looks on their faces. Six days later, however, Bostic was signed by the Washington Redskins, who needed a long-snapper.

"They already had a guy who was a long-snapper," said Bostic, referring to Eagles backup center Mark Slater. "Going to the Redskins was the best thing that ever happened to me." Bostic became a starter with the Redskins, winning three Super Bowl rings and making the Pro Bowl as a member of the most highly publicized line in pro football history, the Hogs. The Redskins thrived on their famed 60 Counter Gap, a misdirection play on which Bostic usually executed a slant block on the defensive right end.

"Jeff was an undersized guy, at most 245-250," said Jim Hanifan, Bostic's line coach in Washington. "But what a warrior. Jeff was one tough guy. Smart as all get-out. With weight training, he got bigger, maybe 265-270. But as the season wore down, he wore down, too. In those Super Bowls, I'll bet he didn't weigh more than 255 at most. He was one tough, smart cookie."

"I saw Dick Vermeil a couple of years ago," said Bostic. "He told me, 'It just goes to show you how smart a coach I am.'"

CARL HAIRSTON

Carl Hairston was shooting pool in a Martinsville, Virginia., hall when Sam Trott approached him. Trott was an alumnus of a small college named Maryland-Eastern Shore and a volunteer football recruiter. All Trott knew was that Hairston was a big man. He assumed that if Hairston was shooting pool, he could handle himself on a football field, given the reputation of Martinsville pool players.

Hairston was then employed as a truck driver for a furniture company, working the Martinsville-to-New York turnpike route for $250 per week. "I had just come off the road and went across the street to the pool hall," Hairston recalled. "Sam asked me if I played football. I weighed about 275 at the time. I had gotten out of high school and had been working for two years. We talked, and two weeks later, he told me I had been accepted at Maryland-Eastern Shore."

With more than wide-open arms, it turned out. Hairston started as a linebacker and defensive end all four seasons that he played. They called him Hurricane Hairston because he blew away the blockers with a quick first step and elusive move to the quarterback. Maryland-Eastern Shore, however, went winless in Hairston's final two seasons. Yet the late Jackie Graves, an Eagles scout, liked his quickness and size. Accordingly, the Eagles took Hairston with their seventh pick, marking the start of an extraordinary career in pro football. Two other defensive linemen, Mike Smith and Greg Johnson, were taken earlier but never made it past their first Eagles camp.

Hairston played 15 seasons (224 games), piling up 94 sacks and making 100 or more tackles five straight years (1977-81). His nickname changed to "Big Daddy," reflecting a warm, caring individual. His school's name changed, too, to Maryland State. By any name, Carl Hairston was a model player, not only for seventh-rounders but for blue-chip first-rounders.

JAY BERWANGER

He will forever be remembered as the first Heisman Trophy winner and the star who chose the business world over pro football. Jay Berwanger was known as "the one-man show" for his dazzling running, passing, and kicking for the University of Chicago. The Eagles made him the first pick of the very first NFL draft in 1936. But Berwanger opted to earn his living in business. "If I had been born 20 years later, it might have been different," Berwanger has said. He retired as an executive in the rubber industry. The Eagles really didn't draft a great player until they hit on halfback Steve Van Buren in 1944. Jay Berwanger died of lung cancer on June 26, 2002, at age 88.

STEVE ZABEL

The years pass by, more than 30 now since Steve Zabel was the Eagles' No. 1 pick in a 1970 draft that also included John Carlos, the Olympic sprinter. "They told me, 'Get as big as you can get, because we want to run the ball,'" said Zabel. "So I came in [as a tight end] at 265. We were so bad. I got kicked out of three games that rookie year for fighting. I was so frustrated. I was playing and I wasn't playing. I got kicked out of the final game against Pittsburgh. Joe Greene jumped off sides seven times. The eighth time, he just picked up the ball and threw it into the stands. My wife was sitting outside the stadium in the car. We had already packed and were going to get out of 'Doag-ee'. She was listening on the radio and heard them say, "There's another fight breaking out... it looks like it's Zabel. He's getting the [bleep] beat out of him.' Five Steelers were whaling away at me, and none of my teammates would help."

The Eagles finished 3-10-1 and would never compile a winning season in Zabel's five-year career, during which he played under three different coaches. In his second year, the Eagles told Zabel they were considering him at three different positions. One option: lose 20 pounds and play weak-side linebacker. Another: keep growing and play offensive tackle. "I was the best offensive lineman they had," said Zabel. "Oh, we were lousy...we were lousy."

A year later, the in-house odyssey of Steve Zabel continued. When the Eagles traded unhappy Tim Rossovich, coach Eddie Khayat approached Zabel and told him, "We just traded Tim. You're our new middle linebacker." Zabel took the news like a true Eagle, digging into his playbook and putting his head on a swivel to cope with the blockers who would now be coming at him from all angles.

"If I had been a different kind of player, I would have said, 'Screw you, I had nine quarterback sacks [as a weak-side linebacker],'" he said. "But I was Mr. Humble. I was just starting to get a grip on what was going on when we lost to the Washington Redskins, 14-0. We bussed back and got in at 2 a.m. Eddie Khayat got us up at nine o'clock and we had a goal-line scrimmage because we didn't score inside the red zone. I tore up a knee. [Defensive tackle] Gary Pettigrew got a hip pointer. [Halfback] Lee Bougess tore up a knee."

They were crippled and overworked. And Zabel says it continued the following year. "We were in two-a-days from July 10 or 11 through September 15," he said. "Nine weeks of two-a-days. We'd have an Oklahoma drill [once called the Nutcracker] every morning to find out who was tough and who wasn't. They had running backs coming and going. That year we were 2-12. I tore up my left knee and my elbow, and the next season, another new coach came in, Mike McCormack."

Zabel was traded to New England, where he played outside linebacker on some fine Patriots teams. He had been a star two-way player at Oklahoma, lining up at tight end on offense and rushing the passer from a three-point stance as an outside backer on defense. Did he ever think about what might have been if he had been a tight end all the way?

"No, I loved defense," he said. "On defense, all you did was instinctive. I couldn't do that as a tight end. Plus, if you're on offense, they want you to put together 17- or 18-play drives all the time. But on defense, it's three plays and get out and get back to the sidelines and cheer. I loved to play defense. I got jazzed up, going out and shutting them down. And I loved standing on the sidelines cheering for the offense."

There was another reason that Steve Zabel loved contact. When he was playing for the Hawks in the Young America Football League in Denver, there was a snowstorm before his first game. "I was a seven-year-old," said Zabel. "After the first quarter, I was freezing. So I went back to the car. I didn't care." The next year, Zabel missed a tackle on a 60-yard run. The play happened to be prominently displayed on the front sports page of the *Rocky Mountain News*.

The next day, Zabel's father tossed a dollar bill on the back lawn and told his son, "If you can tackle me, it's yours." Zabel took several runs at his father, each time slipping to the ground. "I was crying," he said. "Snot was coming out of my nose. My mother was behind the screen door, watching my dad pounding the [bleep] out of me and screaming at us." He finally got it right, dipping for leverage, putting his shoulder into his dad's gut, wrapping up and leaving the elder Zabel sprawled on the ground, not far from the dollar bill. That was the brisk Colorado morning that young Steve Zabel fell in love with defense.

IKE KELLEY

Special teams change, the young toughs of one year becoming the forgotten toughs of the next. But Ike Kelley always remained, from his arrival as a 17th-round linebacker in 1966 until he was released seven years later. He was the perfect kick-cover specialist, a husky 225-pounder who had terrorized the Big Ten as Ohio State's leading tackler.

Kelley would run down under kickoffs with havoc in mind. Sure enough, he was elected to captain the Eagles special teams, thereafter known as Kelley's Killers. His assignment, breaking downfield from the middle, was to take care of the kicker. Usually, this was an easy trick. Most kickers were lightweights and lingered near the tee after the ball was in the air. But not Cleveland's Lou "The Toe" Groza, who had been a Pro Bowl tackle in his earlier years.

"The first time I ran after him, I remember Floyd Peters had sent a telegram to Groza, telling him to 'watch out for Kelley.' Peters had played in Cleveland. The first damn kickoff return we had that day, I didn't realize how big this guy was. He was a straight-ahead kicker, and he came forward and kept his head down. When he raised his head, I was in his chest. I bounced off him like I was a rubber ball. I thought, 'Damn, I got to get him down,' so I cut his legs out."

Kelley's twice-a-year jousts with Lou Groza thrilled Eagle fans. But Groza wasn't the only target. "I remember a preseason game in Baltimore," said Kelley. "Lou Michaels was the kicker. I hit him on the first kickoff. He came over to me after the play and put his arm around me and said, 'Hey, Rook, if you don't block me any more, I won't run downfield. This is only the preseason.'"

A few years ago, Ike Kelley revisited Franklin Field, where he used to meet up with Lou Groza. Their confrontations lasted for only two years. Groza was then 42 and kicking with a leg that had lost its snap. "I enjoyed seeing Franklin Field and the Vet," he said. "The office at 30th and Market, and all the trips over to Franklin for practice. There was just something about the fan base. They were phenomenal. Sixty-thousand strong, either cheering you or booing you. All of the great history there. It was just phenomenal. I truly enjoyed it."

Now, almost 30 years later, Ike Kelly still misses the camaraderie of the dressing room. He has worked as the director of corporate personnel for Worthington Industries in Columbus, Ohio, for 29 years. "It's a steel processing company with 59 locations in the United States and 11 in foreign countries and sales of about two billion dollars," he said. "It was founded by John H. McConnell, who was a ball player at Michigan State. He liked former ball players because he said they were used to getting knocked down and getting back up."

Kelley thought once more about the old gang at Franklin Field, the Eagles' cozy home from 1958-70. "You miss most of all the camaraderie among your teammates, even your coaches," he said. "I don't think you can ever equal that later in life."

CHUCK HUGHES

Chuck Hughes was always described as a whippet, small and wiry with quick moves. "A light, fast greyhound," said Joe Hughes, his older brother. In three years at Texas Western, Hughes caught 168 passes for 2,997 yards. In a game against North Texas State, he caught 10 passes for a whopping 349 yards, averaging nearly 35 yards per catch. Some whippet.

The Eagles, projecting Hughes as a big-play receiver, made him their fourth-round draft pick in 1967. The year before, flanker Ron Goodwin had been the only wide receiver to catch a touchdown pass. Over the next three years, Hughes would fill a backup role, catching six passes and occasionally returning a kick. In 1970, he was traded to the Detroit Lions. The next year, on October 24, 1971, Chuck Hughes collapsed in a game at Tiger Stadium and died after suffering a heart attack. He was just 28 years old.

"He ran down the field, and the ball was thrown to Charlie Sanders," said Joe Hughes. "Chuck fell down. As Sanders was walking back to the huddle, he looked down and Chuck was turning blue. Sanders called to the referee that something was wrong. Chuck actually died of cardiac arrest. I had heard that he had had a heart attack in Philadelphia but they never caught it."

Joe Hughes and Chuck's wife, Sharon, flew to Detroit the next day. "The team doctor told Sharon that Chuck just ran himself to death. I heard that some guys would take pills, Darvon pills, open 'em up and take the green section out and throw the other part away. Then they'd be able to run, run, run. They'd get a lot of pep that way."

The Hughes family of 16 children, it turns out, has had a long history of heart disease. Joe has had two open-heart operations. Another brother, Pat, had a heart attack in Israel. He caught pneumonia from a disinfectant used in his room and died. Hughes' father, an air force pilot, suffered a crushed heart valve in a crash in Goose Bay, Labrador, and died at 45. Their mother died at 52 from a heart attack. A sister, Kathy, lived until she was 70 but also died from a heart attack.

"I never had a heart attack," said Joe Hughes, now 68 and retired in Cherry Hill, New Jersey, where Chuck lived when he was an Eagle. "I came back from Saudi Arabia one time and just wasn't feeling well. I was diagnosed with high cholesterol. We all had high cholesterol. There are only 10 of us left. We're going fast."

Joe Hughes misses his football-playing brother terribly. He has talked to old Eagles and old Lions, and what he hears only confirms how special his younger brother was.

"Chuck was one of those guys who was very well-liked," he said. "For example, I was in Detroit, coming down the elevator with Charlie [Sanders]. I asked him about Chuck. He said, 'He was one of those guys who always had a kind word for you. He was never in a big hurry.' I talked to the equipment guy. He said that when the guys would come off the field and needed their cleats cleaned, Chuck used to say, 'I'll do it.'"

Joe Hughes told the story of the time Sanders received a bolo tie in the mail from some fan. "Anybody want to wear something like this?" said Sanders, waving the western-style tie in the air. "I will," said Chuck Hughes.

"He died doing what he liked to do," said Joe Hughes. "He never became a cripple from it. That's the way I look at it. After Chuck died, they called him the Titanic of football."

Following Hughes' death, pro football began paying more attention to heart problems, cholesterol levels, and any strange-looking pills in the dressing room.

BOB PELLEGRINI

They were rowdy and they were good. They weren't the most talented team in the league, but the 1960 Eagles swaggered through the season and won a championship that should have been won by the Green Bay Packers or the Cleveland Browns.

If this was a heist, and it was, then Bob Pellegrini was the big man who made sure there was no trouble with the getaway. Pellegrini was a great linebacker at Maryland. He was listed at 6-foot-2 and 233 pounds, but in appearance he looked taller and bigger. And certainly fearsome, with his size, his dark eyes and his cutting insults. Jack McKinney, a fine *Philadelphia Daily News* sports columnist who sometimes liked to mix it up himself, referred to Pellegrini as "The Cop." Pellegrini played the role, using his fists and his mouth against anyone who tangled with anyone in an Eagles uniform.

"I'll tell you, the camaraderie we had took up for anything we lacked in talent," said Pellegrini. "We'd all meet on Mondays at Donohoe's, a bar at 62nd and Walnut. Dutch [quarterback Norm Van Brocklin] would drop his kids off about 9:30 or 10 o'clock, and we'd be there all [bleeping] day. One day [Chuck] Bednarik got so incensed he got all over Jim McCusker. Another time, Billy Ray Barnes and Jack McKinney got into it. But we'd always come together. We'd help each other out."

Pellegrini was usually the first to arrive at the scene of a fight. He remembers playing the Baltimore Colts in a benefit basketball game. Gene "Big Daddy" Lipscomb slammed into Bednarik, a collision that presumably shook the gymnasium. Pellegrini began shouting insults at Big Daddy Lipscomb, moving in like a heavyweight with a haymaker to throw. Indeed, he threw one that decked Colts linebacker Bill Pellington. "[Jim] Mutscheller was holding me, but I broke away and nailed the [bleep] out of Pellington," said Pelly. "He went down like a kite. He needed 12 stitches above his eye. He was a dirty, rotten punk. He went into Bednarik and I dropped him. I used to say, 'C'mon, let's start something.' Hey, the more brazen you are, the less you've got to fend. Each of us has his forte. Bednarik was a preacher. I was a good fighter. I loved it."

Philadelphia Daily News sports columnist Jack McKinney refered to Bob
Pellegrini as "The Cop." Pellegrini played the role, using his fists and
his mouth against anyone who tangled with his teammates.

The Eagles trained in Hershey, the chocolate town, located about 100 miles from Philadelphia. Their favorite bar was Martini's, just down the road from the Community Center, where the players stayed. "The owners were John and Annie Martini," said Pellegrini. "I'd hang out there and got to know them really well. One time we played an exhibition game in Richmond and got back at two in the morning. John gave me the key out the window and we went in and drank the rest of the night. We'd leave the money on the bar."

In one of his adventurous moods, Pelly once stole a wooden Indian from the local park. The idea was to use the Indian as a dummy so he could hang out at Martini's long after bed check.

"It was wooden, or maybe plastic," he said. "One night Jurgy [Sonny Jurgensen] stole it and put it in his room. Then I got nailed. They called in the FBI to look for the Indian and somebody put it on the elevator and pushed the button. When the door opened on the first floor, all hell broke loose."

Pellegrini still raves about the feeling the Eagles had for each other during that magical season. Yet, while there is respect for Bednarik, the legend of them all, there is also a sense that Bednarik has turned his unique two-way role into something bigger than life.

"He only played one game full-time," says Bob Pellegrini, referring to Bednarik's 58-minute championship game against the Packers in 1960. "I got hurt [against the New York Giants] and he took my place. If I didn't get hurt, he didn't play [linebacker]. I pulled a groin. It was one of the few times I couldn't go. In the second half, he played center and linebacker and that was the day he hurt [Frank] Gifford."

Bob Pellegrini was either the second or third pick in the 1956 draft, depending on whether you count quarterback Gary Glick, a bonus choice by Pittsburgh. "I got a $3,000 bonus and a $9,000 salary," he said. "And I had to kiss [general manager] Vince McNally's rear to get that. I figured the difference between me and Donovan [Eagles quarterback Donovan McNabb, the No. 2 pick in the 1999 draft] was about $54 million."

KEVIN REILLY

Kevin Reilly got the idea from a photo he had seen of Larry Csonka and Jim Kiick, the Miami backs. They had posed as Butch Cassidy and the

Sundance Kid, a backfield dressed as outlaws of the night. Reilly figured that the seven Eagles linebackers could pose, too, and look like ruffian cowboys.

"We all grew beards," recalled Reilly. "The last day of training camp, before the photo was taken, we all had to chug 16-ounce cans of Coors to seal the oath. We were a very close-knit group. You thought it was normal until you got older, and then it seemed abnormal to find guys that special. They called us Bergey's Boys [middle backer Bill Bergey was the acknowledged ringleader]. The photo was published in the October 6, 1975 issue of *People* magazine. It was a pullout, two pages. Henry Kissinger was on the cover."

Reilly, who was Bergey's backup, logged a lot of special-teams minutes. "They once introduced me, saying 'our own Kevin Reilly,' because I was from Villanova," he recalled of his rookie season. "They introduced the special team that day. I just got chills. I floated across that AstroTurf." Late in the 1974 season, he began to feel pain in his left shoulder. Suspecting bursitis, the Eagles treated Reilly with a series of cortisone shots. He played another season, hustling on special-teams units and banging the enemy with his aching shoulder. Finally, when the pain persisted, Reilly decided to retire before the 1976 season.

His shoulder problem went with him. A year later, they discovered a tumor known as a desmoid in his left shoulder. A desmoid tumor, while considered benign because it does not metastasize, or spread, to other parts of the body, is extremely painful. It usually arises in the muscle sheath and ties or binds the nearby organs. Though Reilly's doctors tried to save his arm, they couldn't cope with the tough, hard fibers of the desmoid. "It's a low-grade form of cancer," said Reilly. "It's a form of keloid, which black persons sometimes get after a fracture. The skin raises up and there is a lot of scarring. The desmoid never stopped growing."

In 1979, Kevin Reilly underwent an 11 ½-hour operation at New York's Sloan-Kettering Hospital to remove his left arm and shoulder, three ribs and his collarbone (a similar operation on former San Francisco pitcher Dave Dravecky in 1991 took only two and a half hours with the aid of laser treatment).

"They saved my life," said Reilly. After the operation and after the last tube had been removed, the day came for the thick bandage wrapped around Reilly's left side to be removed. Reilly tried to brace himself for what he would soon see in the mirror, his left side without any arm or shoulder. The wait seemed interminable.

Kevin Reilly, once a backup Eagles linebacker and now a motivational speaker, lost his left arm and shoulder after developing a tumor in his left shoulder.

"They wanted John [Bunting] to be there," he said, referring to a fellow linebacker. "They told me John and Rene Bunting were coming to take me out to dinner." Reilly and Bunting entered the bathroom, where the bandage was slowly removed. They were both shocked, neither wanting to reveal the mental pain of the moment to the other.

Reilly uses his ordeal as the theme for up to 75 motivational speeches he was scheduled to deliver in 2002. His audiences range from administrators to high schoolers. He also works for Xerox as a marketing manager. In his inspirational talks, Reilly challenges his listeners to never be beaten by the odds. "I'm loud, I'm dynamic," says Reilly, who demonstrates how he can knot his tie with his teeth. "I tell them not to listen to people and not to place limitations on themselves," he said. "I read them little poems. And I use a little humor, like Lou Holtz."

He once met Rocky Bleier, the old Pittsburgh Steeler, who is also a motivational speaker. "He gave me a little advice," said Reilly. "He said, 'Don't quit on anything unless you've tried it three times.'"

JOHN REAVES

He threw beautiful spirals, just as he had done in college, the ball rotating tightly through the air. But the pro game was different. Not only were the cornerbacks and pass rushers quicker, but those defensive coordinators who wig-wagged in the sets were more clever. Especially when they sensed that John Reaves was his own worst enemy in the huddle.

"I didn't have a very good feel for the game back then," said Reaves, the Eagles' No. 1 draft pick in 1972. "Quarterbacks called their own plays. I never called a play in my life. I really didn't know much about defenses. I was really a babe in the woods. I remember one time I called a reverse. I came to the sidelines and the coach, Coach [Ed] Khayat I think, said, 'We don't call reverses in that situation.' I said, 'Really?' I didn't know. It was just something that just popped in my head."

At Florida, Reaves passed for 7,549 career yards, then an NCAA record. He put up that number despite playing his final two years under Doug Dickey, who used a split-veer option attack. He had this classic, overhead delivery and nimble drop-back. The Eagles, who had gotten only 13 touchdown passes from Pete Liske and Rick Arrington the year before, shoved Reaves into the starting lineup, hoping he was a fast learner.

"I was a young, brash 22-year-old who didn't know what he was doing," he said. "I played five games with a fractured ankle, torn ligaments. That limited my mobility. I feel kind of unfulfilled. I'm really disappointed in my pro career. I wish I had had an opportunity to do well. But I never had anybody tell me about coverages. About how to attack defenses. I got to where I could call plays after a few years."

But by then, Reaves was a third-stringer, eventually swapped to the Cincinnati Bengals, a team that collected quarterbacks. Then it was Houston and finally back home to the Tampa Bay Buccaneers. He mopped up in two games for the Bucs, and his NFL career was over.

No longer that babe in the woods, Reaves resurfaced with the USFL rival Tampa Bay Bandits and threw for 4,092 yards and 28 touchdowns in his second season. His play caller was a coach named Steve Spurrier.

RICK ENGLES

It started out as a routine training camp competition. But by the end of the 1978 camp, it became a soap opera titled *As the Punters Turn*. The competitors were Rick Engles and Mitch Hoopes. Here's how the soapy went. The Eagles cut Hoopes on August 15. They cut Engles on August 22 and brought back Hoopes. They cut Hoopes on August 28 and brought back Engles. They cut Engles on September 25 and brought back Hoopes. Finally, they cut Hoopes once more on September 30 and hurriedly dispatched an aide to Chicago, where Engles signed a contract just before the 4 p.m. deadline.

Engles kicked for six games. The soap opera then turned into a scary adventure. On his own, Engles ran out of punt formation in the opener, then threw a pass that lost two yards in the fifth game. Coach Dick Vermeil, angry and frustrated, sent him packing. His successor was Mike Michel, a free agent from Miami. But that wasn't the last the Eagles heard from Engles. Later that season, Engles claimed he and Hoopes had been "stashed," or hidden in a nearby hotel after being waived. "I've lost my wife and I'm broke," Engles said. "She took all of the money and filed for divorce." Engles said that after he was cut, the Eagles "paid all of my expenses—food, laundry, phone bills—everything. Mitch told me he rang up about a $500 bill. He really lived it up."

The Eagles shuffled Engles from one hotel to another, once registering him under the name of Rick Bengles. Indeed, I remember Engles sitting next to me at the counter of a Ramada Inn in suburban Essington, Pennsylvania. He ordered a breakfast of steak and eggs two days after being waived. Asked how long he planned to stay in the area, Engles smiled. "Oh, I'm going to hang around here for a while," he said. "It's a long drive to Oklahoma, and I'm in no hurry."

Vermeil denied he had stashed either punter. Stashing, or hiding waived players, was a common practice before the salary cap made it impossible. Yet stashing a punter was considered a sign of desperation. "What we were guilty of was paying his expenses for one week when he was not on our active roster," said Vermeil. "I lost confidence in the guy, but I couldn't get anybody better. My players didn't have any confidence in him. When I got a chance to get somebody better, I got him." The league eventually confirmed that Engles had indeed been stashed and took away the Eagles' third-round pick in the 1980 draft. The Eagles that year could have drafted wideout Carlos Carson, who caught 353 passes in his career for the Kansas City Chiefs.

GREG BROWN

The odds were staggering. Greg Brown was working on a construction crew in Washington, D.C., earning $10.50 an hour. He had played two seasons as a pass-rushing end at Kansas State, then transferred to that football power, Eastern Illinois. Married in high school, Brown quit football after one semester to take care of his family. But then a strange and abrupt and wonderful meeting took place. John Teerlink, the line coach at Eastern Illinois, had moved on to the University of Illinois and was on a recruiting trip. Teerlink stopped at an intersection and happened to recognize Brown. They shared dinner that night, and Teerlink later called an old friend, Chuck Clausen, the Eagles' defensive coach. On Teerlink's recommendation, the Eagles offered Brown a free agent contract. His bonus was $1,000.

"I didn't get my hopes up," said Brown. "I realized it was a long shot." Even longer than the Eagles imagined, because Brown showed up as a 220-pounder, about 30 pounds under his college weight. Bulking up on a steak-and-shake diet, Brown muscled his way to 249 pounds and became an Eagle. When the defensive line was riddled by injuries, Brown emerged as the starting right end in a 3-4 alignment. A few years later, he collected 16 sacks, beating up on some of the league's best tackles. The Eagles rewarded him with a generous three-year, $1.5 million contract.

"I guess I was in the right place at the right time," Brown said. "I went in at the right time and got it [the contract] done." Brown, of course, was referring to his signing that took place about a month before Norman Braman bought the Eagles from Leonard Tose. The contract angered not only Braman but 11 of Brown's teammates, who refused to report to camp in 1985. The next year, the Eagles hired Buddy Ryan as head coach. Ryan switched to a 4-3 defense and traded Brown to Atlanta, where he was reunited with Marion Campbell, his Eagles coach. Brown produced two sacks in two years. His "million-to-one" career, as he put it, was over. "I never saw a longer long shot in all of my years in football," said Chuck Clausen. "But I also never saw a guy who wanted it more."

And whatever happened to Leonard Mitchell, the 6-foot-7 defensive end picked on the first round of the 1981 draft? Mitchell was flopped to offense in 1984, then traded to Atlanta in 1987. He started for a bad 3-12 team and then was cut. Greg Brown, his old competitor, outlasted him in years, sacks, and money.

JOE PISARCIK

There was always a crowd around Joe Pisarcik's locker. But the overflow of media types was always turned the other way, toward the adjacent locker of fellow quarterback Ron Jaworski, the most quoted player in Eagles history. Pisarcik, who possessed a great arm but little mobility, started only three games in a five-year career as a backup quarterback, preparing but almost always sitting.

"Being with Dick Vermeil, he made you feel that you were important to the team," said Pisarcik. "Even though I was a backup, he still made me feel good about myself." Pisarcik also had a unique perk. In 1981, the year after he was traded to the Eagles by the New York Giants, he signed a four-year contract. The first three years were guaranteed, a rare concession to a backup.

"At that point, I was probably the 11th-highest paid quarterback," he said. "I was paid better than some of the starting quarterbacks. I was with a team that had just gone to the Super Bowl and was in my option year. Dick said he wanted me to stay. They almost doubled my contract. So, financially, I knew I was set. It was guaranteed in case of injury, illness, or death."

The money was good for Joe Pisarcik. Indeed, in 1982, he earned a base of $175,000, more than starters Vince Evans of Chicago ($170,000), Bill Kenney of Kansas City ($130,000), Neil Lomax of St. Louis ($130,000),

Doug Williams of Tampa Bay ($120,000), Tommy Kramer of Minnesota ($100,000), David Woodley of Miami ($100,000), and Eric Hipple of Detroit ($62,500). Yet there has always been that wonder within Pisarcik's mind of what might have been under different circumstances. Jaworski, the guy in front of him, had been All-Pro and Player of the Year and had taken the Eagles to the Super Bowl. So what if Pisarcik and his receivers put on a midweek show? This was always Jaworski's offense, to run and talk about.

"I can tell you now that I had a better arm than he did," said Pisarcik. "You could see that when we practiced every day. Dick saw it but didn't want the players to make any comments." Pisarcik came off the bench to win two games in his first four seasons, once going eight for ten for 101 yards and one touchdown in the 1983 season opener against San Francisco, the Super Bowl champion. He started the final three games in 1984 when Jaworski broke his leg. By then, Vermeil had retired, replaced by Marion Campbell.

"The next year, which wasn't guaranteed on my contract, I asked Marion Campbell to tell me the truth about my future," said Pisarcik. "He said, 'Joe, we're going to keep you.' I had been through two minicamps. I had told them that if they were going to cut me, cut me then. The day before training camp, they cut me. All the moves had been made. All the trades had been made. All the draft picks had been made."

There was a brief fling with Miami after Don Shula called Dick Vermeil, who raved about Pisarcik's arm. Then Joe Pisarcik decided to retire at 33. Of course, his name will always be remembered for the last-second Miracle of the Meadowlands fumble that devastated the Giants in 1978. When Pisarcik came to the Eagles, he took a ribbing from some of the Miracle of the Meadowlands cast.

"Sure, [Bill] Bergey and Herm, they got on me," he said. "That's just the way we were. I hear about that play during every week of my life. What people forget is that I fell on the ball [to kill time] on the first play when we got it back. Then the coach sent in the play. I wondered what they were doing. I tried to hand it off and then boom...boom...boom." Edwards scooped up Pisarcik's hurried handoff that glanced off Larry Csonka's hip and ran 26 yards for the miracle touchdown with 31 seconds left.

The Giants coaches were fired for the gaffe. Their names have been forgotten, except when one of them uses the bizarre play to open a little banquet speech. Joe Pisarcik has emerged as the punching bag for Giants fans with long memories and anyone else who wants a laugh on a rainy Sunday morning in November. Pisarcik, of course, deserved better, but quarterbacks are always the fall guys, aren't they?

LEROY HARRIS

Leroy Harris, the doughnut-loving fullback, caught only 15 passes in 1980, most of them little swings and screens. But one of them was much more than a flip. Trailing the Oakland Raiders in a defensive struggle, 7-3, the Eagles were desperate for a big play. Ron Jaworski, under pressure from a blitz, shook loose from linebacker Randy McClanahan's grasp just long enough to spot Harris standing all alone near the other sideline. "I'm supposed to be just a decoy," piped Harris, who caught Jaworski's desperation pass for a 43-yard gain. Seven plays later, Wilbert Montgomery scored for a 10-7 win. The Eagles needed it for the home-field advantage in their successful drive to the Super Bowl. "It's amazing he caught that pass," said coach Dick Vermeil. "He drops so many easy ones on the practice field where he sometimes is like a volleyball player."

Unfortunately, the career of Leroy Harris ended almost before it began. He shocked his teammates in 1983 by testifying in a child support hearing that he spent part of a $60,000 bonus on drugs. "Well, I'm a junkie," he told a juvenile court judge in Camden, New Jersey. Friends, however, said Harris, a man of shifting moods and weight, made his statement as an attempt to keep from paying support to his wife, Shirley. Whatever the plot, Harris passed a drug test a month later, then was cut by the Eagles. "I like to munch a lot," said Harris, who sometimes hit 242 pounds on the scale. "But, hey, I'm not the only one. Everybody goes to that doughnut table." His favorite: a chocolate-glazed double-doughnut sandwich.

SEAN LANDETA

Sean Landeta was eight years old when Baltimore kicker Jim O'Brien won Super Bowl V with a pressure field goal. "When the Colts won that year, me and every other kid in Baltimore wanted to pretend we were the guy who won the Super Bowl," Landeta recalled. "We all went outside every day and practiced kicking a football over an old volleyball net, pretending we were kicking it through the goal posts."

Yet Landeta didn't begin formal punting until he was a senior at Loch Raven High School in Towson, Maryland. "As I was leaving after my senior photo was taken, the football coach happened to be walking down the

The 2005 season marked Sean Landeta's 21st season in an NFL jersey, and his fifth with the Eagles.

corridor," said Landeta. "He asked how my summer vacation was going. Then he asked me about coming out for the team." That was the start of a remarkable professional career that has lasted 21 years, the last 17 as one of the NFL's most consistent punters.

Few, if any, pro athletes know more about their position than Sean Landeta. He can tell you with historical authority about Sammy Baugh's booming quick kicks. And about Horace Gillom's hang time. Or Tommy Davis' consistency and punting angles. "Tommy Davis for the 49ers had a 10-year stretch that was just phenomenal," he said. "Yale Lary, to be such a great defensive back and to punt that way was quite amazing. And think about Sammy Baugh, a defensive back, a quarterback, and a punter for the Redskins. Horace Gillom of the Browns, I think he was the first punter to stand 15 yards behind the line. Before that, they stood 10 yards back. It's just been interesting how the position of the punter mirrors the changes in the game."

Two new rules in 1974 changed the concept of punting. The goal posts were moved from the goal line to the end line. On missed field goals from outside the 20, the ball was returned to the line of scrimmage rather than the 20-yard line. "Before 1974, a punt was almost never tried from plus 50 [inside the 50-yard line]," Landeta said. "It was totally different."

Landeta, the historian, can also explain why the old coffin-corner punt has become virtually obsolete. "Some guys still do it," he said. "But the reason you don't see it as much is plain and simple. If you took 10 shots at punting the ball, it's easier to lay it up rather than kick for the corner. When you lay it up, or pooch it, as they say, a couple of things can happen. The returner can muff or fumble the ball with three or four guys around him. If the ball hits around the 10-yard line, it doesn't always bounce into the end zone. So it's simple. You have a better percentage laying it up."

In 2001, his 17th year in the league and third with the Eagles, Landeta boomed 97 punts for a solid 43.5-yard average. That made him the all-time NFL leader in career punts (1,216) and punting yards (52,737). "If I hadn't met the coach that day, I might never have played football," Landeta said wistfully. "What if the photographer had taken a few more shots? What if I had hit a red light or two driving over? It was totally by accident."

TERRELL OWENS

Terrell Owens was a disliker. He disliked Brad Childress, the Eagles' bright offensive coordinator. He disliked Donovan McNabb, the Pro Bowl quarterback. He disliked the creative game plans drawn up by Andy Reid, the head coach.

Except, of course, when Reid fed Childress a clever play from the plan and McNabb fed T.O. a touchdown pass. Then Owens was a liker, a smiler, a strutter, a prancer, and a dancer, who ran to the nearest TV camera after the catch.

Owens came to the Eagles in 2004 following a complex, three-team trade, His original seven-year contract was worth a whopping $48.724 million, including a $2.3 million signing bonus; a $6.2 million roster bonus and a $660,000 base. "All he has to do is keep his mouth shut for three years and he gets $21 million," said one agent at the time.

T.O. quickly developed a cult-like following. From the moment his first training camp opened, they screamed his name ("T.O.! T.O.! T.O.!"), louder and longer than they screamed for Donovan McNabb. Owens responded with a magical first year. He caught 77 passes, 14 of them for touchdowns, despite suffering a high ankle sprain and broken fibula in the 14th week.

Owens made an amazing recovery to play in Super Bowl XXXIX. He caught nine passes despite the pain and New England's strong secondary play. Yet, there were signs that T.O.'s time in Philadelphia was about to end. When McNabb, reflecting on the team's depth and versatility, said he felt the Eagles could reach the Super Bowl without him, Owens began to rant about others and rave about himself.

The low point in his second year came in mid-season when he made his 100th career touchdown catch. Owens said the Eagles showed "a lack of class" by not honoring him on that historic day. Then he let McNabb have it. In the same interview, Owens claimed the Eagles would be an improved team with Brett Favre at quarterback.

At that point, with the Eagles struggling with a 4-3 record, Reid had had enough of Owens' cutting lines. He suspended T.O., then deactivated him for the final five games. The next year Owens was gone. As one agent told me, "He picked the wrong fight here."

There is no debate about the receiving skills of the 6-foot-3, 226-pound, ego-driven Owens. In 22 starts as an Eagle, he caught 133 passes and scored 20 touchdowns. The Eagles were 17-5 in those games. Owens, on the other hand, also verbally assaulted three quarterbacks: San Francico's Jeff Garcia and Tim Rattay and, of course, McNabb.

But now Terrell Owens is gone. Yet, not completely out of sight. T.O. now plays for the Dallas Cowboys, a despised NFC East opponent coached by taskmaster Bill Parcells. Will he survive in Dallas? Will he connect with quarterback Drew Bledsoe?

"This is Amereica's Team," said Owens soon after joining the Cowboys. "I feel right at home. I'm a star among stars now."

The Eagles got a laugh out of that line. Indeed, the team seemed looser and tighter as it headed into Reid's eighth training camp. The screams for T. O. had ended. There was a new kid in Owens' spot, Reggie Brown, poised to create his own screams.

Most importantly, there was harmony in the player ranks. And as we all know, except perhaps for Terrell Owens, winning always starts in the mind.

DAVID AKERS

David Akers, the best kicker in Eagles history, has made 83 percent of his field goal tries, a lot of them in tricky stadium winds. He holds most of the Eagles' kicking records. He's made the Pro Bowl three times.

Yet Akers still insists that he still feels insecure after all those big years. "There are different insecurities," says Akers, a four-team journeyman who joined the Eagles in 1999. "You always have to prove something. First, you prove to somebody that you're good enough to play in the NFL. Then you prove that you're worthy of a contract. And then you've got to prove that you're worthy of that contract."

In 2005, Akers' seventh season with the Eagles, he missed four games with a torn hamstring in his kicking leg. Akers made only 16 field goals in 22 attempts, or 72.7 percent of his tries. Before that, he had been near-perfect, 139 of 165, or 84.3 percent. They called him Automatic Akers, or Green Akers if you watched ESPN, which loves those nicknames. The tear happened in the second game. Akers responded to treatment and kicked off against the next week.

"It just tore," he said. "It partially came off the hip bone, I guess. Some people read the MRI a little differently. They said it would take a year to get the feeling back, to get pain-free. But I came back sooner."

Kickers are usually little guys, with cold nerves and enormous power in their legs. Akers is that kind of guy, 5-foot-10 and cool inside a rowdy stadium. His size doesn't reflect the power and muscle in *both* legs, the right plant leg and the left kicking leg. The serving wrists of tennis players are usually larger than the opposite wrist. But Akers says the muscles in his plant leg, are larger than in his left leg.

"You might think it's weird, but I generate a lot of my power my right leg," Akers said. "I plant with my hips and put it through. So I'm actually a little bit stronger in my right leg. If you've got an ACL (anterior cruciate ligament) injury, it's longer for a kicker coming back from that on his plant leg because that's where all the torque comes from."

Akers is a workout warrior. His off-season consists of long days of Brazilian jiu-jitsu and other kicking arts with two Philadelphia trainers, plus regular team workouts. Yet, after another leg-weary day, Akers admits that the mental side is the toughest part of the game.

"There are a lot of college guys who are very, very talented physically," he said. "But they just can't put it all together. You have to get the ball off much faster in the NFL. And the ball (in the NFL, new, slick balls known as K balls are used for kicking) doesn't go as far."

Akers was a 152-pound freshman at Louisville when he began kicking. He matured into a decent kicker and was signed by Carolina in 1997. He couldn't beat out John Kasay that year. After a brief stop in Atlanta, Akers had his chance in Washington but missed two field goals in a close game and was cut. In 1999, he turned up in Philadelphia, where he would erase most of Paul McFadden's kicking records (e.g., points in a season; 133; career field goals, 155; consecutive field goals, 17; through 2005). It was almost as if the Eagles got even (see Jeff Bostic).

How powerful is Akers' leg? He once made a 72-yarder in some forgotten Eagles training camp practice. ("The balls were older at the time, before they started using the K balls.") He tried a 65-yarder at Louisville that struck the right upright. His longest pro kick has been 57 yards.

"He has a chance to become the best kicker in the history if the NFL," said special teams coach John Harbaugh. Akers, the perfectionist, won't go that far. "For me," he said, "anything less than 100 percent, I'm settling for mediocrity."

BRIAN WESTBROOK

Howie Long…Joe Klecko…Billy (White Shoes) Johnson…Mike Siani. They were all backyard prospects: Long and Siani from Villanova; Klecko from Temple, and Johnson from Widener. The Eagles passed on all of them on draft day, missing out on three Pro Bowlers (Long, Klecko and Johnson); a Hall of Famer (Long) and a solid starter (Siani).

Atoning for these sins of decision, the Eagles took a Villanova running back named Brian Westbrook on the third round of the 2002 draft. Forget that Westbrook measured 5-foot-8—on all of the scouting charts. Or that he played at a I-AA school. All coach Andy Reid knew was that Westbrook had produced some magical numbers (NCAA-record 9,885 all-purpose yards; 84 touchdowns; 4,499 rushing yards; 2,639 receiving yards, and four touchdowns on kickoff returns).

"The Eagles are going to be shocked at what they have," said Villanova coach Andy Talley after Westbrook got the call from Reid. "He can do everything—run, catch, and return. He's a rare talent."

There are always an army of little wiggle guys like Brian Westbrook who arrive in training camps with big numbers like that. But Westbrook has proved to be everything that Talley said he would be and everything that Reid hoped he would be.

"It's disappointing that people still have that opinion that small guys can't get it done," says Westbrook, who is generously listed at 5-10 on the roster sheet. "I think some of the better players in the NFL were small guys. But people, they just have hangups with people that are small."

Before Westbrook arrived, the Eagles' most feared runner was their quarterback, Donovan McNabb. Then Westbrook began to accelerate through the holes created by a big, veteran line. Reid also began flexing him outside as a receiver, and Westbrook began catching in bunches. He caught 73 passes in his third season, when he emerged as the perfect fit for Reid's West Coast offense. Reid loves to throw the ball. Last season, his pass-run percent ratio was 64.5-35.5.

"In the Senior Bowl he was the quickest guy on the field," says Reid. "He played physically. He had one shot at a linebacker and just about killed the guy. You look at those things."

For as far back as he can remember, Westbrook has always been the quickest kid in the neighborhood and in school. "I've always been pretty quick," he said. "Quick with the first step, you know?"

Quicker than Allen Iverson, the city's basketball star? "Well, it's different sports," said Westbrook, who was quick enough to play point guard at DeMatha High (Hyattsville, Maryland), a schoolboy basketball power. "But he [Iverson] is very quick in his arena. I think I'm pretty quick in my arena as well. We should have a little contest to see."

Some backs are surprised by their moves when they see themselves on tape. Not Westbrook. "You add a little more [moves] every year," he said, "but a lot of the things are the same moves I've been doing for a long time. So seeing them doesn't amaze me as much as it amazes other people."

Wilbert Montgomery, the team's all-time rush leader, was small, too, listed at 5-foot-10, 194 pounds, but really smaller than that. Yet Montgomery carried the ball a lot more in a balanced attack. In their first Super Bowl season (1980), the Eagles were almost perfectly balanced: 49.1 percent passes; 50.9 percent runs. Despite missing four games, Montgomery carried the ball 193 times that year. Westbrook's highest total is 177 carries in 2004, the Eagles' second Super Bowl appearance.

"I think our offense has the capability to run the ball a lot more," he said. "But that's up to Coach Reid. I just play it by ear with that. In the Super Bowl, I think we got away from our game plan a little bit." The Eagles did. Trailing by only 14-7 early in the third period, Reid called 31 pass plays and only six runs, five by Westbrook.

The Eagles will continue to come out throwing as long as Andy Reid is the head coach. Westbrook will get his "touches," as they say, but it will be a fight to get 1,000 yards, the number linked to the Pro Bowl, sizable bonuses, and other perks of the game.

Brian Westbrook has the moves. He's always had those. He just wants the ball in his hands like the league's other wiggle backs.

4

THE COACHES

MIKE McCORMACK

In the summer of 1974, Mike McCormack made a speech to his players that he never expected to make. With a preseason strike looming, McCormack wanted to make sure there was unity in the ranks. "I told them that whatever they decided to do, they'd better stay together," said McCormack. "I was pretty adamant about that."

Despite McCormack's emotional plea, the Eagles were a divided house. When the players struck while union head Ed Garvey was waging a court fight for free agency in Mackey v. NFL, there were 20 Eagle strikebreakers and 28 strikers. Among those who crossed the picket lines were quarterback Roman Gabriel and middle linebacker Bill Bergey.

"They were the two lightning rods," said McCormack. "Gabe and Bergey were the stars. A lot of guys resented that they had gone to Mexico in the off-season with Leonard [owner Leonard Tose]." With the strikers walking the sidewalks around West Chester State, McCormack tried playing little mind games. The idea was to rave about some specific free agents, hoping to flush out the veterans from the picket line.

"When Atlanta came in to play, we came in by bus through the gates and that's all I remember," said McCormack, whose teams was jeered by striking

Mike McCormack had to deal with striking players and a team divided during his tenure on the Eagles sidelines in the 1970s.

players and NFL Players Association reps waving picket signs. "Van Brocklin [Falcons coach Norm Van Brocklin] and I got together at the 50-yard line and talked about how crazy it all was." The Falcons romped, 23-7. Later, the equipment managers noted that some jittery starters on McCormack's patchwork team had handed in damp jockstraps.

The Eagles never recovered from the summer strike. They finished 7-7 in 1974, then 4-10 in 1975, and McCormack was gone. His '74 team could easily have gone 10-4. Marion Reeves fumbled away a punt against Dallas, setting up a decisive touchdown. Tight end Charle Young stepped out of the end zone, nullifying a touchdown against New Orleans in a 14-10 squeaker. A blocked punt and a crucial fumble by Gabriel cost another win against Washington.

Yet despite an overall 16-25-1 record (11 losses by 45 points), Mike McCormack still speaks highly of his years as an Eagle. "I think Philadelphia is an outstanding place to coach," he said. "I've said it many times that when you're coaching the Eagles, at the start of every game they're your fans. They may not be at halftime. But no matter what happens the week before, they're your fans. Coaching there prepared me for a lot of other things. After three years there, you don't think anything can happen that will affect you. You know you've been hardened to everything."

EDDIE KHAYAT

Three losing games into the 1971 season, the Eagles were in turmoil. They were young and thin in the ranks and they had been outscored, 110-24. General manager Pete Retzlaff promptly fired head coach Jerry Williams and turned to defensive line coach Eddie Khayat, a former teammate, to salvage the season. Khayat, a big bear of a man with a southern drawl and a taste for long cigars, figured that his first step was to restore discipline.

The day after a misty-eyed Williams conducted his final interview in a South Philadelphia diner, Khayat announced a ban on all facial hair. "It was not a big deal," Khayat said. "It was not the first time that had been done. I had talked to some of our veteran players the day before. Too many of our guys wanted to do their own thing. I wanted them all to get alike very quickly. I told them what I planned to do. To a man, they said to do it."

However, some black players who desired facial hair disagreed with Khayat's directive. Their quotes ended up in the local papers, accompanied by headlines the size of those for Khayat's hiring.

Eddie Khayat, who played on the 1960 Eagles championship squad, coached the Eagles in 1971 and 1972. As a coach, Khayat is best remembered for his ban on facial hair.

"It was blown out of proportion," said Khayat, a tough defensive tackle on the closest group in Eagles history, the 1960 championship team. "A lot of teams operated exactly the same way." Khayat likes to tell the story of Mel Tom, a quiet but playful defensive end.

Tom approached the coach one day with a towel covering half of his face. "Coach," said Tom, "I know you're willing to meet people half-way on this." Tom then pulled the towel away. "He had half a mustache," said Khayat, breaking into a laugh. "No, they took it in stride. Hank Stram had the same rules. Lombardi had the same rules. I knew I needed to shake things up a little bit. The whole purpose was to bring everybody together."

Khayat also coached along military lines. Somebody once handed him a copy of General George Patton's famous hell-raising speech. "It was similar to the one in the movie, only they cleaned that one up a little," said Khayat. "I must have been 22 then. I thought it pertained to football. How important every person's job was. In the military structure, you had to have teamwork. In New England, I remember Raymond Berry coaching up there. I don't know if I've ever seen a better example of teamwork. The lady running the computers, she'd run off to school and drop off her two daughters. Then she'd come flying into the office as a sign of how together they were. No, you can't compare football with war. But with the whole structure, there are a lot of similarities."

The clean-shaven Eagles, by the way, rallied to post a 6-2-1 record to finish at 6-7-1. The next year, they were riddled by injuries and plunged to 2-11-1, saved from a winless season by two one-point wins. Khayat was dismissed. "I still have some fond memories of my tour of duty there," said Khayat, using the military term.

DICK VERMEIL

The euphoria from winning the Rose Bowl with an underdog UCLA team had barely subsided when Dick Vermeil headed east. He had grown up in California's Napa Valley wine country and climbed the playing and coaching ladder on the West Coast. Suddenly, though, a couple of easterners named Leonard Tose and Jim Murray were in his life, offering Vermeil more money than he ever dreamed about to coach the Philadelphia Eagles.

Tose was the club's flamboyant owner. Murray was his general manager, confidante, and constant traveling companion. They became equally euphoric after seeing Vermeil carried off the field by the biggest of the Bruins after their Rose Bowl upset. Tose and Murray were staying at the swank Beverly Hills Hotel. Murray peeled off enough $100 bills, known to wheeler-dealers as crackbacks, to extend their stay in two three-bedroom bungalows. Indeed, Tose's bungalow had been reserved for Yitzhak Rabin, the Israeli Prime Minister. But the power of the dollar got Tose his lodging.

"We've got squatters' rights," said Tose as Murray eyed several of Rabin's guards, who were carrying Uzis and dressed in camouflage colors. "Tell them I won't buy any more Israeli bonds."

A little Mexican servant would pick up the party's dress suits each day. He would see Tose and Murray and sing out, "I keek a football for you."

As Murray recalled, Vermeil arrived in a powder-blue Mustang, UCLA's colors. "Dick got over there in about eight minutes," Murray said. "Later we found out his father drove race cars. It was a very intense interview. He told us he would be back. We had to wait another week before we closed the deal. He was our guy."

Tose had interviewed Joe Paterno, the popular Penn State coach. Murray had interviewed Allie Sherman, the former New York Giants coach. "Joe stayed up all night, writing all of his requests on a yellow pad," said Murray. "Leonard, of course, doesn't have any attention span. He just glanced for a few seconds at Joe's pad and said, 'Anything else, Coach?' Joe turned as white as the table napkins."

Vermeil got the job with a unique contract. A kicker clause that rewarded him with a percentage bonus of every dollar he saved, membership in a country club, a new car, life insurance and health benefits, and a promise from Jim Murray. "If the Philly fans accept you," Murray said, "you'll be a household word."

"I think I was sort of overwhelmed initially with the magnitude of the job," said Vermeil. "You know, coming from UCLA, where you had all the best players once you got going. Then all of a sudden, you come in and take over a losing organization. I felt very insecure. My routine was always just try to work harder. You know, see if I could catch up that way."

Vermeil started training camp on July 3, 1976, at the height of the city's bicentennial celebration. The next night, while he was conducting a team meeting at Widener College, Vermeil was interrupted by a Fourth of July fireworks celebration. He ordered Carl Peterson, his administrative assistant, to "go outside and tell them to hold the noise down."

The Eagles lost six straight preseason games, scoring 70 points. Vermeil had no running game. The quarterbacks were Mike Boryla, a streaky 50-

Dick Vermeil came to Philadelphia from UCLA in 1976 and had the Eagles in the Super Bowl by 1980. Vermeil retired from the Eagles at a misty-eyed ceremony in 1983, then came back and led the Rams to a Super Bowl in 2000.

percent passer who struggled with his rhythm, and Roman Gabriel, who was past his prime. But Vermeil soon found he had a bigger problem.

"There were a lot of innuendos about the team and drugs and cocaine, all that kind of stuff," he said. "When I came in there, I was going to make sure we cleaned that element out of there. It wasn't hard to get the information we needed to do that. It came from information from former players on other rosters. I don't know if it was widespread, but there were individuals involved. But that wasn't unique to the Philadelphia Eagles. The whole league was going through a transition period. They didn't have any policies. There were no testing programs. That was an era rather than just the NFL. I got rid of the guys that I thought were involved. Three or four of them, not many. It was common practice. Not for you or me, but for that element and that age group. The college campuses, everywhere."

By the third year, Vermeil had turned over half of his starters. He made a great trade to get unhappy quarterback Ron Jaworski from the Los Angeles Rams and made two super-lucky picks to get defensive end Carl Hairston at No. 7 in the 1976 draft and halfback Wilbert Montgomery at No. 6 in the 1977 draft. In Vermeil's fifth season, the Eagles made it to their first Super Bowl, feeding off their coach's work ethic. They finished 12-4, losing four games by a total of 22 points.

Despite the presence of comedian Don Rickles in the Superdome dressing room, invited there by Tose, the Eagles seemed tight and restless before Super Bowl XV. They were beaten by the Oakland Raiders, a haunting defeat that would not be personally avenged until Vermeil won the big one with the St. Louis Rams 19 years later. By then, Vermeil had retired from the Eagles at a misty-eyed ceremony in 1983. He returned to coaching with the Rams in 1996, then retired again after winning Super Bowl XXXIV. Peterson, who was then running the Kansas City Chiefs, persuaded Vermeil to make yet another comeback. But what about his wife, Carol, and her belief that a husband should take time to enjoy the fragrance of summer roses and the dazzling colors of autumn leaves ?

"She was not a factor," said Vermeil. "She did not want me to retire. She is for me doing what I love to do. I love being involved in it, the coaching and the players. It's the only thing I know how to do in a competitive way."

Vermeil coached the Chiefs for five seasons but was never able to build a defense to match his high-scoring offense. He retired after the 2005 season in which the Chiefs led the league in total offense but finished 25th in defense, living up to their reputation.

ANDY REID

As far back as high school, Andy Reid knew he wanted to coach the sport he loved to play. "You know, you're thinking of what you want to grow up to be," he said. "You're thinking about it, but I didn't take that direction initially in college. I kind of went through the premed route. Then I hit that organic chem [class] and I went, 'Maybe I'll be a coach.'"

Reid played up and down the offensive line at Brigham Young, protecting a free-spirited quarterback named Jim McMahon. "I was a very average player," he said. "I was fortunate to be able to play every position. I was small, about 240 pounds. But I could run; I could do five [seconds] flat. I've put on a good 100 pounds. I tell my wife that she got twice for the money."

Owner Jeffrey Lurie also got a formidable coach for his money when he hired Reid off Mike Holmgren's talented Green Bay staff in 1999. "The players see him for what he is, which is an honest, hardworking, obsessed with winning, good guy," says Lurie. "He always does what he thinks is best for the team, not what other people are clamoring for."

Andy Reid accepted almost every imaginable challenge in his early coaching years. He learned to build cabinets. He salvaged antique cars and made them run again. He even cranked out a sports column for the *Provo Daily Herald* while at Brigham Young. His summer training camp and his seasonal workouts reflect a remarkable attention to detail and organization.

Sean Landeta, the Eagles' 40-year-old punter, remembers how Reid, then coaching the quarterbacks, used to linger when the Packers worked on their kicking game. "Some of the other position coaches would watch, too," said Landeta. "But he really took an interest. I said to myself, 'You know, this guy watches everything.'"

After three seasons in which Reid turned a 3-13 team into an 11-5 division winner, the Eagles appear poised for a Super Bowl run. "We're not necessarily man for man the most talented group in the league," admits Reid. "But our guys have a great attitude. They're good guys, but on the field, they're nasty and play hard. And I think that's important."

Reid played with the same intensity. "Yeah, maybe it reflects me," he said, laughing at a memory that was in the air, "except that they're better than I was. Thank goodness I'm not playing."

On the brink of their Super Bowl run in 2004, the Eagles signed Terrell Owens, a tall, acrobatic wide receiver who liked the ball in his hands on every other play. It was the worst mistake of the Reid era. Reid had repeatedly struggled to find enough skilled receivers for his West Coast offense. Owens gave him big plays. But he also gave Reid trouble, a lot of trouble.

After catching nine passes in the Super Bowl loss, Owens swaggered through the ranks, criticizing players and coaches alike. Reid finally had enough and dismissed Owens from the roster after the 2005 season for, as the coach put it, "a large number of situations that accumulated over a long period of time."

With Owens gone and a new crop of receivers on the field, Reid faced a new season in 2006 with guarded optimism. "I have great leadership on the team," said Reid. "Those guys know what they need to do. And there are no hangovers from last year.

"It's a fresh start to get yourself right and go."

JOE KUHARICH

During the final game of the 1967 season, an old crop-duster plane flew over Franklin Field with a trailing banner that read, "Goodbye Joe Baby." The flyover was plotted by the Committee to Rejuvenate the Philadelphia Eagles, a 500-member card-carrying group dedicated to banishing coach Joe Kuharich to some foreign outpost. Outside the stadium, fans were implored to deposit official Joe Must Go ballots into the bowels of a colonial era outhouse.

Kuharich, the son of Yugoslav immigrants, coached one more season. The Eagles, riddled by Kuharich's trades of receiver Tommy McDonald, halfback Timmy Brown, cornerback Irv Cross, tackle Bob Brown, linebacker Maxie Baughan, and quarterback Sonny Jurgensen and his mishandling of key players, finished with a 2-12 record, losing 11 in a row. Owner Jerry Wolman fell, too. Wolman, a 36-year-old whiz kid in the construction business, bought the Eagles for $5.5 million in 1963. But when his company made a $20-million mistake on a Chicago insurance tower, he filed for bankruptcy and lost the Eagles. Kuharich, the most unpopular coach in Eagles history, became part of the collapse.

Kuharich left behind a drab 28-41-1 record and a lot of odd quotes that crossed with his humorless personality. A sampling:

"Football is a tough game; you win some, you lose some, and some you teeter-totter."

"Trading quarterbacks is a rarity but not unusual."

"It's a horse of a different fire department."

"A missed block here, a missed assignment there, it all adds up. It's happened to teams before," (after losing to the Dallas Cowboys, 56-7).

"When the gods of the gridiron don't smile on you, you're in trouble."

"The players have got to learn that they shouldn't read about what Joe Bananas says about them in the press."

Despite Kuharich's gobbledygook and his ongoing feud with the Philadelphia press (he frequently refused to appear for Monday morning press conferences), Wolman gave his coach a whopping 15-year contract as general manager and a four-year coaching contract. Kuharich also got an option to buy into the club. He simply rehired himself after the fourth season, which ended with him sticking out his tongue at a dozen tormentors in the Franklin Field stands.

Kuharich was a football man all the way. Born in South Bend, Indiana, he used to loiter near the Notre Dame practice field, where Knute Rockne was coaching his great teams. "By the time I entered high school, I had already made up my mind to play football and then to coach it," he once said. "The fact is, I never wanted to be anything but a football coach."

Even then, as a schoolboy perhaps dreaming of coaching the Irish, which he did (he was to become the only Notre Dame coach with a losing record) Kuharich could never have imagined signing a 15-year, $900,000 contract with a pro team. There were unfounded reports that commissioner Pete Rozelle forced Wolman to hire Kuharich as a condition for purchasing the Eagles.

Whatever the deal, Joe Kuharich remains the most scorned figure in Eagles history. During his stormy coaching career, fans wore "Impeach Kuharich" buttons and featured "Joe Must Go" stickers on their car bumpers. Kuharich's players used to listen to his weekly radio show and burst out in laughter at his double-talk.

Kuharich once announced an unusual tactic after the Eagles had won the coin toss. If the kickoff return was to the 20-yard line, King Hill would start at quarterback. If it went to the 40-yard line, Norm Snead would start. But if the return went to the opponent's 40-yard line, Jack Concannon would start. Kuharich always liked to be an original. He considered players to be interchangeable, accounting for his no-star system.

"He was the worst coach I ever played for," said Timmy Brown, who spent half his career in Kuharich's dog house. "I hate the guy with a passion."

There was another side to Joe Kuharich that fans never realized until he became very sick with cancer in 1980. Vermeil had hired Kuharich as a low-key aide. "I can still see Joe, who loved to talk, walking around the track in training camp for hours, telling the people about his doctor and his treatment," said Jim Murray, the general manager.

Kuharich died on January 25, 1981, on the morning of the Eagles' Super Bowl. "When I last visited him at Graduate Hospital," said Murray, "he was asleep. But I decided to wake him. He went into a locker-room speech, about us winning the Super Bowl. He just did this beautifully." Murray, sensing that Kuharich was close to death, leaned over and kissed his old coach on the cheek. "All right, maybe he wasn't as successful as other coaches," said Murray. "But he was a guy with a heart bigger than Franklin Field, where he coached."

NICK SKORICH

They handed Nick Skorich a championship team, minus its quarterback, inspirational leader and, some teammates said, its coach. That would be Norm Van Brocklin, the Dutchman who led, passed, and sometimes coached the 1960 Eagles to their third national championship.

But Skorich knew that Sonny Jurgensen, a fifth-year quarterback who understudied Dutch, had a great passing arm. And there was Timmy Brown, the young runner; Bobby Walston, the clutch kicker, and Pete Retzlaff and Tommy McDonald, the receivers, along with Chuck Bednarik and most of the defensive heroes from the title year.

"I took over in '61," said Skorich, who ended a 50-year pro career in 2002 when he retired from the league's officiating department. "We had a good team. Jurgensen became the quarterback. We were 10-4 but lost the Eastern Conference by a half-game [to the New York Giants' 10-3-1 record and last-week 7-7 tie with Cleveland]. That put us into the Runner-up Bowl. That was the deciding factor that broke the team up."

The Eagles were routed by a tough Detroit defense that included Alex Karras, Roger Brown, Joe Schmidt, Wayne Walker, Dick Lane, and Yale Lary. The casualty list was stunning. "Jurgensen got a severely separated shoulder," said Skorich. "He had to have an operation where they pinned it down. That wiped him out for two years. We had about four or five key injuries and we were never the same. The replacements we got were very slow. That [championship] team was never deep in reserves. There were 22 guys who kept us going. We suddenly disappeared."

Nick Skorich got the job that some say should have been Norm Van Brocklin's, taking over the defending champion Eagles in 1961. Skorich lasted three seasons, and the Eagles went 5-20-3 in his final two.

So did Skorich, after 3-10-1 and 2-10-2 seasons. "Sonny Jurgensen was a great quarterback," Skorich said. "He proved that in Washington a couple of years later. He became a big star in the league and a Hall of Fame quarterback."

The story is told, or maybe the rumors were told, that Van Brocklin was supposed to succeed Greasy Neale as head coach in 1961. "I think Van Brocklin at that time expected to be the head coach," said Skorich. "[General manager] Vince McNally interviewed me, and I was hired a week or so later. The contract was for $25,000. I'm not sure if Van Brocklin had already taken the Minnesota job or not."

Nick Skorich would remain in coaching until 1974, a career that included four years (and a division title and two playoff appearances). He played, too. Skorich was a Pittsburgh Steelers guard from 1946-48. "I was a 200-pounder," he said. "But we ran Jock Sutherland's single-wing attack, with an unbalanced line. We had a tailback, a fullback, and a blocking quarterback. In that type of offense, I could play at 200 because I was quick and strong and I could trap."

JERRY WILLIAMS

Over the years, you remember the hard losses and the sad times longer than the epic triumphs and the Sunday night celebrations. That's the opinion of Tex Schramm, who used to run the Dallas Cowboys.

I was shopping in Princeton, New Jersey, when I learned that commissioner Pete Rozelle had died. I saw Jack Youngblood with his head pressed against a towel, fighting back tears after the favored Los Angeles Rams had suffered a crushing playoff loss to the Minnesota Vikings. And there was the moving funeral service in a hushed New Orleans evening for Jim Finks, a fine husband and football man. Yet the saddest I have ever felt for another human being was in late December 1971. Earlier that year, Jerry Williams had been fired by Eagles owner Leonard Tose after a dismal 0-3 start. Williams had openly wept the next day in the booth of a South Philadelphia diner, where he gave his farewell interview.

Williams was an air force lieutenant who flew P-38s in the Pacific theatre during World War II. "I flew 26 missions and came back on every one," said Williams, who continued flying as a hobby during his coaching career.

The Cleveland Browns were fighting for a playoff spot in 1971 with their Bill Nelsen-Leroy Kelly-Gene Hickerson team. Their head coach was Nick

In Philadelphia, fans remember Jerry Williams as the secondary coach of a defense that held the Packers to one touchdown in the 1960 title game, rather than the head coach Leonard Tose fired after an 0-3 start in 1971.

Skorich, who had been an assistant with Williams on the Eagles' 1960 championship team. Skorich, of course, knew all about Williams' defensive wrinkles, including the use of extra backs, a tactic that evolved into George Allen's nickel defense. But he desperately needed somebody to coach his receivers. "I didn't have a receivers coach," said Skorich. "Jerry was a solid coach who did a good job of getting his point across to the players. We had a lot of injuries and were turning over new receivers every week. He was looking for a job, so I said 'C'mon in.'"

Williams lived alone in a downtown hotel room that December. There were Christmas lights in the lobby and bells ringing in the streets near the shoppers. Williams seemed melancholy when we talked that night following practice. He was misty-eyed as he reflected on his sudden firing. As Tex Schramm says, you remember the defeats and the setbacks, and the memories of failure can leave a grown man, even a heroic fighter pilot, in tears.

In Philadelphia, however, they remember Jerry Williams as the secondary coach of a defense that held the Packers to one touchdown in the 1960 title game.

SID GILLMAN

Off the field, Sid Gillman was never far from a film projector. He studied and learned about the passing game like Picasso studied life with a brush in hand. Gillman used his imagination to develop the sophisticated pass offense that is such a big part of pro football in the 21st century.

Extra receivers. The comeback routes. The use of backs running routes upfield. These tactics are so familiar today. But in the '60s, that kind of passing style was uniquely Gillmanesque. He coached the Eagles on three separate occasions, working for Dick Vermeil in 1979-80 and 1982 and for Marion Campbell in 1985.

"The first time we lived in the Society Hill Towers, right across from Bookbinder's," said Esther, Gillman's wife. "I used to tease [owner] John Taxin. I told him that when I was cooking, or doing the dishes, I could look out and tell how much business they were doing. They used to have tour buses lined up there."

In Gillman's second tour, they lived in an apartment at 2400 Chestnut Street. "We came back when Marion Campbell took over," she said. "I always loved to walk. I'd go out to the campus at the University of

Pennsylvania. I had a knee replacement and can't even walk a half-block now."

Gillman turned 90 in 2002. He and Esther moved from a luxury home just off the first hole at the famed La Costa golf course to Century City in Los Angeles. Gillman is confined to a wheelchair but exercises regularly. "I've been exercising for a long time," he said. "I do some weight-lifting and all kinds of things. It's very intense. I've got a girl who helps me during the week."

Esther Gillman says her husband became interested in obtaining a projector to view football films when they were dating in the early '30s. "We'd go to the theatre where they would show these Grantland Rice sports reels before the movies," she said. "Something flashed through his brain, and he had his brother tell the projectionist to snip the football parts off the sports reels and send them to him. Before we left on our honeymoon, he was looking through the want ads and saw a 35-millimeter projector on sale for $15. He bought it and I gave him hell. I told him we couldn't afford to buy a projector when his first job was going to pay him $1,800 a year. He'd pin a sheet on the wall and run that projector, using the sports clips that his brother would send. The colleges didn't have any equipment like that. Sid introduced them to the use of film. He was way ahead of himself in the use of visual aids."

The worst part of his coaching stints in Philadelphia came in 1982, Dick Vermeil's last year. The players struck for 57 days, nearly wiping out the season. Vermeil, Gillman's longtime coaching friend, quit the Eagles because of coaching burnout. During the strike, the coaches would prepare game plans, uncertain when the walkout would end.

"We didn't go back to California; we stayed right there," recalled Gillman. "I never thought we would lose the season. The thing I recall is that we had enough opponents [nine] left to play the season."

The Gillmans moved to Los Angeles to be closer to two of their children. "We've been married for 67 years," says Esther Gillman. "If you counted it down with his time away from me, it wouldn't even amount to 50." She laughed easily, a woman still deeply in love with her 90-year-old husband, the guru of the passing game. Bill Walsh gets credit for developing the popular West Coast offense. But his teacher was Sid Gillman, when he was younger and fascinated by analyzing one of those passing films.

Sid Gillman, who was elected to the Pro Football Hall of Fame in 1983, died in 2003. He was 91.

MARION CAMPBELL

Marion Campbell almost always had the horses. The Carl Eller-Alan Page-Gary Larsen-Jim Marshall line at Minnesota. The Deacon Jones-Merlin Olsen-Rosey Grier-Lamar Lundy line in Los Angeles. The units even had nicknames. The Vikings' Purple People Eaters. The Rams' Fearsome Foursome.

In those early coaching years, Campbell was a coordinator, plotting defensive strategy and turning loose those powerful rushlines. Years later, he would return to Philadelphia, where he had been an All-Pro defensive tackle on the Eagles' 1960 championship team. And when Dick Vermeil retired, Campbell was bumped up to the head job. He had changed from a 4-3 traditionalist to a 3-4 coach, a system where the rushline occupies two gaps, allowing the linebackers to flow to the ball. Campbell's line included Dennis Harrison, a 6'8" end, Kenny Clarke, a journeyman nose tackle, and Greg Brown, literally signed off the streets. By the time a new pass-rusher named Reggie White arrived in 1985, Campbell was on his way out. Yet he still has a fondness for the city.

"I still love Philadelphia," said Campbell. "It's a great professional city all the way around. I loved the people up there. I loved playing there and loved coming up there."

If the city's slogan means anything ("The City That Loves You Back"), then Marion Campbell and Philadelphia still have a torrid love affair going. At least the old-time Eagles watchers, who still remember Campbell as a tough, intense defensive tackle in the 1960 title game.

"We were very close," said Campbell of the '60 team. "It was a bunch of smart people. Football-smart people. They were intense players, mentally and physically. We weren't overloaded with coaches. We didn't have that many. We had to do a lot of it ourselves. One thing we really were. We were unselfish. Our coach was Buck Shaw. He was tremendous at moving guys around. The championship game, you knew it was going to be close. A struggle up and down the field. But we felt comfortable all along. You could just see in our faces that we weren't going to lose."

Despite the Eagles' success and Campbell's All-Pro form, the big contracts didn't come easily for him. The team negotiator was Vince McNally, a tough man across the table. "We'd stare at each other for what seemed like an eternity," said Campbell. "I would get my raise, but it used to take a while. But he was a good man. God rest his soul."

Marion Campbell, All-Pro defensive tackle on the Eagles' 1960 championship team, took over as the Eagles head coach after Dick Vermeil retired in 1983.

Marion Campbell is now 73. But it wouldn't matter if he was 20 years younger. He doesn't think he could coach under today's liberalized free agency/salary cap system. "You're not able to keep all of those free agents any more," he said. "The 49ers, the Redskins, I just don't think you could keep it going like they did. I don't think Pittsburgh would have won all of those Super Bowls."

Under free agency, the Fearsome Foursome would have been reduced to the Fearsome Twosome. And Marion Campbell finds that very sad.

GREASY NEALE

They say a team reflects the personality of its head coach. The Green Bay Packers and Vince Lombardi, the whip-cracker. The San Francisco 49ers and Bill Walsh, the offensive genius. The Dallas Cowboys and Tom Landry, the innovator. But few, if any, teams reflected the dynamic personality of a coach more than the Eagles' two-time championship teams in 1948-49. Their coach was Earl "Greasy" Neale. "A tough cob from the steel mills in West Virginia," said Al Wistert, the All-Pro tackle. "But a wonderful man. He started coaching when he was still in high school. He had been around for years. When somebody made a mistake, you'd learn from it. You'd give him an idea and he'd take it. He was educated in the steel mills, but he was smart."

So smart, in fact, that he actually coached his high school team in Parkersburg, West Virginia, to a state championship. So smart that he pulled off the first "naked reverse" while coaching at Washington and Jefferson. So smart, or maybe just nervy, that he played 60 minutes for the Ironton Tanks in 1930 on a dare when he was 39. The Tanks upset the Portsmouth Spartans, an NFL team, 16-15.

Neale was also a skilled outfielder with the Cincinnati Reds, batting .357 in the infamous 1919 World Series against the Chicago Black Sox. He was a man for all sports, often moonlighting during his baseball years with the Canton Bulldogs. But his greatest fame came during the Eagles' dynasty years, 1944-49, when they went 51-17-3 and won back-to-back championships.

Owner Lex Thompson, a Yale man, lured him off the school's staff to coach the Eagles in 1941. He became fascinated with the T-formation, spending long nights analyzing the Chicago Bears on film. Neale also originated the so-called Eagle defense, a 5-4-2 scheme in which linemen sometimes dropped into pass coverage. Sure, that's the same tactic used in the modern zone blitz package, which so many current coaches claim to have created.

"We used the 5-4-2 except when we played Jock Sutherland's Pittsburgh teams," said Wistert. "That was a single-wing team. So we used a slanting line. Maybe a looping line is a better way to describe it. We drove them nuts. We'd always loop, either inside or outside. It fouled up their blocking assignments."

Neale was a world-class bridge player and often played cards or golf with his players. "Greasy had a dual personality, which to me is what a successful coach must have," said center Alex Wojciechowicz in Myron Cope's reflective book, *The Game That Was*. "He's got to be a no-good son of a gun on the field and a great guy off the field."

"I lost my father at an early age, and I always wondered what I wanted him to be like," said Wistert. "I'm sure now it would have been like Greasy Neale. During my eight years I played for Greasy, I never told him how I felt because I always wanted to make sure in my mind if I ever slipped, sentiment wouldn't make Greasy keep me in the lineup. He was a rough cob and I wasn't used to that kind of person. Then I began to understand him."

Neale was both a driver and a father figure, mixing discipline, confidence, and smarts. He was one of the most versatile of all pro athletes and probably could have made a living in football or baseball, or maybe golf if he had worked at it. But he drove himself hardest of all at becoming a coach. During those dynasty years, 1944-49, the Eagles outscored their opponents by an average score of 26.5-14.7. The Eagles achieved eight shutouts in their 1948-49 title seasons. They were Greasy's boys, as the coach called them, the kings of pro football.

JERRY WAMPFLER

Jerry Sisemore, the undersized tackle, was one of those yes-sir, no-sir guys. Long on effort and skill, but short on quotes. He played 12 seasons for the Eagles, five of them under the firm hand of Jerry Wampfler, the line coach.

"He was the best technician I ever had," said Wampfler. "He was the best technically sound player I ever coached. Jerry was tough. But his toughness was not a demonstrative toughness. He never cheap-shotted anybody. When somebody put a little cheap-shot on him, he wouldn't say a word. But he had a calculating mind. He'd wait and then kick the [bleep] out of the guy."

Wampfler and Sisemore got along because the player believed in Wampfler's driving style and the little kick-step technique that was so much a part of his blocking package. But not every lineman bonded with Wampfler. In 1973, incoming head coach Mike McCormack hired Wampfler and John Sandusky, two talented offensive line coaches. Wampfler got the defensive line job because his players were more experienced. One of them was Mel Tom, a moody end from Hawaii.

After taking some heavy criticism at practice one day, Tom came right out with it. "Fight me, trade me, or fine me," Tom yelled, staring at Wampfler, who began laughing. "Mel, you're not worth any of the three," he said.

Sure enough, Tom was gone the next season. But Sisemore, the leather-tough Texan selected at the top of the 1973 draft, started for the next 12 years. Wampfler returned to coach him in 1979.

"I remember they drafted Leonard Mitchell, a big defensive tackle who couldn't make it and was moved over to offense," said Wampfler. "In the off-season, I was working with Mitchell, who was 6-foot-7. Jerry was there and I remember him saying, 'That's what your new offensive tackles are going to look like.' The surge with bigger people was just coming. The 6'7", 320-pound guys, they could lean on someone and get away with it, and it didn't require as much technique."

WALT MICHAELS

Old linebackers never quite forget the basics. Except, of course, when they're in the middle of a tense game and instincts take over, a moment in which the backer reacts to his gut feeling and ignores the old book of keys and reads.

Walt Michaels was one of those tough, relentless linebackers when he played on those great Cleveland teams. He coached for three seasons in Philadelphia, tutoring a linebacker set of Bill Bergey inside and Frank LeMaster and John Bunting outside. Michaels still marvels at Bergey's style, which was often the instinct-and-guts style.

"He sometimes didn't know why he was doing it, but it was right," said Michaels of Bergey's aggressive play. "And as long as he did it right, it was fine with me. He was a competitor, a hitter, all of those things. He was just unpredictable. But sometimes linebackers have to play like that. Once in a while, you get a freelance runner, and the play is designed to go inside. But he goes outside. And sometimes the linebacker reacts on his feelings and makes the play."

Michaels suggests that neither Bergey, nor Bunting and LeMaster, got the proper recognition for their linebacking play. "Maybe not individually," he said. "But that was circumstances. What four guys were in front of them? You'll find the really good ones have the lines that make it easier for them to make plays, like an LT [Lawrence Taylor]. They can freelance. Bergey had that special hitting ability. The other guys played totally with their heads."

Ironically, Michaels was coached by legendary Paul Brown, who later coached Bergey with the Cincinnati Bengals. "Paul wouldn't allow a lot of the things that Bergey did," said Michaels. "We had to play it right down to the rules. But linebackers sometimes have to react on their instincts, go against the book."

Walt Michaels was a natural linebacker and linebacker coach. He was raised in the Pennsylvania coal country in a town called Swoyersville. When he retired from coaching, he returned to his country roots, settling in a one-bank town called Shickshinny. "I thank God for the guy who invented canes," says Michaels, who underwent neck surgery and lost some of his balance. "But I'm hanging in there. If we divide our lives into four quarters, I'm into the fourth quarter. I'm in the country where there are rural roads. They named one after me, Michaels Road in Shickshinny."

BUCK SHAW

In Buck Shaw's first year, the Eagles won only two games, upsetting the conference champion New York Giants and beating the lowly Chicago Cardinals. Shaw, a quiet silver-haired man of detail, fumed over the final game, a drab 20-0 loss to the Washington Redskins.

"Gentlemen," said Shaw in the silent dressing room, "take a good look around this room at your teammates. It's the last time most of you will see one another."

True to his word, Shaw shuffled the deck. The Eagles traded for Norm Van Brocklin, a hot-tempered quarterback. They drafted halfback Ted Dean, linebacker Maxie Baughan, and safety Don Burroughs. They plucked halfback Timmy Brown in a waiver deal, converted running back Pete Retzlaff to tight end, and elevated Tommy McDonald to starting flanker. They wound up with center Chuck Bednarik doubling as a linebacker in a 60-minute iron-man role. "Buck was strictly low-key," Van Brocklin once

Buck Shaw, right, led the Eagles to the NFL championship in 1960, then retired to enter the business world as an executive with Georgia-Pacific Corp., the paper products firm.

said. "He never raised his voice or lost his composure. He never used profanity. He left that to guys like me."

Shaw, however, gathered up his emotion at the start of each training camp. "Buck told us, 'Some of you guys have All-Pro reputations,'" said Retzlaff. "'But the 33 guys who stay here will be the ones who work the hardest. This team has been a loser for three years now. I could do that well with 33 rookies.'"

With the arrival of Van Brocklin in 1960, the Eagles came together, bonding into a team of fierce passion. They kept winning for Shaw, who played tackle on Notre Dame's great Knute Rockne teams in the early 1920s. Yet as the Eagles were rolling to a 10-2 record and then edging Vince Lombardi's Green Bay Packers for the title, there was a feeling, real or imagined, that the real coach was Van Brocklin. "We knew we were never out of a game as long as we had Dutch," said Tommy McDonald, the little receiver. "He always came up with the big play." Not only executing it but designing it.

"We were like a pack of dogs," said Van Brocklin. "Each one was from a different alley. But we had a helluva good time." Said Bednarik: "What we did that season was a miracle. We weren't that great. The Packers were a great team. They became a dynasty. But on the day we played, we were better."

Shaw retired after winning the title. "Too many people hang around too long," he said, "What if I fell flat on my face? Wouldn't that be a helluva way to wind up 38 years of coaching?" Van Brocklin retired with him, presumably to succeed Shaw as head coach. Instead, the job went to Nick Skorich. Van Brocklin bolted to Minnesota as head coach of the expansion Vikings. In their second year, the Vikings upset the Eagles, giving Van Brocklin a measure of revenge. By then, Buck Shaw was in the business world as an executive with Georgia-Pacific Corp., the paper products firm.

BUDDY RYAN

You've got a winner in town. That was the favorite line of Buddy Ryan, who loved to feed the media a lot of those sound-bite quotes. Ryan molded that great Chicago Bears defense that allowed only 198 points in the regular season and only one touchdown in three playoff games, including Super Bowl XX, in 1985. Ryan's swarming defense earned him the head coaching job the next year in Philadelphia.

And, indeed, Ryan did produce a winner. The Eagles went 10-6, 11-5, and 10-6 in Ryan's final three seasons. Yet after three straight playoff losses, Ryan was fired and headed back to his 676-acre horse farm (500 of the acres are leased) to raise another crop of Kentucky-bred yearlings. What persuaded owner Norman Braman to replace Ryan with likeable Rich Kotite was a series of conflicts that splintered the team's image, if not its chemistry.

Ryan's nervy deeds: (1) He presented player personnel director Joe Woolley and assistant to the president George Azar with "scab rings" for assembling a replacement team during a 24-day players strike in 1987; (2) In 1986, he called club management "stupid" for refusing to allow first-round pick Keith Byars to room by himself during off-season workouts; (3) Ryan, seeking any kind of motivational edge, repeatedly insulted players for missing plays and being "too damn fat;" (4) Sometimes he shuffled starters like a casino dealer, using another of his favorite lines, "His ass is out of here"; (5) He drove quarterback Ron Jaworski crazy by using him on first and second downs, then sending in backup Randall Cunningham on third downs; (6) Ryan also engaged in running feuds with Dallas coach Jimmy Johnson and Braman's close friend, Miami coach Don Shula.

After all of Ryan's needling and knocking, the Eagles emerged in 1988 as a team of hell-raisers that lived by the flying forearm and the Ryan creativity. Braman, the owner, liked the swagger of his team and the wins that Ryan's defense produced. But when the Eagles began playing out of control, Braman remembered how Buddy Ryan had insulted Don Shula, his favorite coach, and Ryan's ass, too, was gone after the 1990 season.

"We had a Super Bowl team there, no doubt about it," said Ryan. "The thing that hurt was that playoff [a 21-7 home loss to the Los Angeles Rams]. Our offensive line got beat up two years in a row. We had to make a lot of changes. We needed a few more drafts to help the offensive line."

Ryan, who owns 15 thoroughbreds and 200 head of cattle on his bluegrass farm, admits to feeling unfulfilled after the playoff failures. "Well, yeah," he said. "I thought that we needed just one more draft to get it done." The pain was softened during the past two years. One son, Rex, won a Super Bowl ring with Baltimore. He coached the Ravens' defensive line. Another, Rob, earned a Super Bowl ring with New England. He coached the Patriots' outside linebackers. "So we've got five Super Bowls in the Ryan family," he said. "I've got three. They've each got one."

He laughed when the issue of his firing came up. "He [Braman] just came down and said they wanted to go in another direction," said Ryan. "That's the old standby line. It's so full of bullshit. But everybody uses it...going in another direction." His successor was Rich Kotite, the man Ryan hired to pep up the Eagle offense in 1990. The hire surprised Ryan. "I didn't think the players respected him that much," he said.

Buddy Ryan says he misses most of all the humor and mood of the locker room. "I talk to my boys all the time," he said. "I've got the NFL [television] package, so I watch a lot of games. I miss the camaraderie in the locker room. Forty-five guys coming together."

Ryan laughed again. "I don't miss bullshitting you guys," he said.

RAY RHODES

Coaches and quarterbacks. Quarterbacks and coaches. During the four seasons that Ray Rhodes coached the Eagles, he never had a quarterback who grabbed the job and refused to let it go. Rhodes opened with Randall Cunningham in 1995 and closed with Koy Detmer in 1998, the dreadful 3-13 finish to his coaching career in Philadelphia.

Rhodes' quarterbacks threw 59 touchdown passes and 71 interceptions in 64 regular-season games. That Rhodes was able to rouse the Eagles to back-to-back 10-6 seasons was something of a miracle considering the Cunningham-to-Rodney Peete-to-Koy Detmer-to-Bobby Hoying shuffle. Indeed, in Rhodes' final season, Hoying failed to throw a single scoring pass in seven starts. Yet Rhodes talks as if the team's downfall was his fault.

Through the 2002 season, Rhodes had coached in 328 games, with a winning record of 206-120-2. In all of his coaching losses, the worst occurred in the 1998 opener. Seattle, coached by Dennis Erickson, crushed the Eagles at home, 38-0, the most humiliating loss in Ray Rhodes' 21-year NFL career. "That was the worst I've ever felt," said Rhodes. "They really outcoached me. I was thoroughly outcoached that day. They had plays from a defensive standpoint that we didn't have an answer for. We studied tapes through the whole preseason and the zone blitz package didn't show up. We tried to go with 'max' protection and we still couldn't get anything done." How did Rhodes try to handle it? "I didn't go out and try to find some booze," he said. "I just tried to restudy things and how they happened."

Rhodes remembers his two early teams, too. The ones that went 10-6 but were ousted in the NFC playoffs. "The '97 team had a strong mix of young players and veterans," said Rhodes. "The team didn't jell as quickly as we thought it would." Rhodes recited the names. Bill Romanowski, Kurt

Gouveia, William Fuller, and Michael Zordich on defense; Raleigh McKenzie, Guy McIntyre, Steve Everitt, Ed West, and Ricky Watters on offense. "We had a strong nucleus of veterans and leaders. We had leadership. We had a nice blend."

But they started to leave. Either out of choice as free agents, or out of necessity because of age. And Rhodes, who coached with passion and cutting words to back it up, never could stabilize the quarterback position. At the end, there were only three remaining starters from his first team: linebacker William Thomas, right corner Bobby Taylor, and strong safety Michael Zordich.

"Quite naturally, anytime you get released it's the low point of your life," said Ray Rhodes. "But this is a business. It's all about winning games."

When the losses began mounting despite Rhodes' fire-and-brimstone style, the coach's children tried to lighten his mood, suggesting he have his ears pierced. "I had one pierced," admitted Rhodes. "It's just something I did for them but not during working hours. I never came to work showing any pierced ear."

Ray Rhodes, a tenacious coach who often talked the language of a dock worker, deserved a better fate. Without a quarterback, however, he had no chance of "putting this team on top," as owner Jeffrey Lurie had said at Rhodes' hiring.

5

THE OWNERS

JERRY WOLMAN

"**W**hen I was a kid, I had one big dream," said Jerry Wolman. "I wanted to own the Eagles, just like some kid hopes to grow up to be Babe Ruth, or the president. Buying the Eagles was like tying my childhood to my adult life."

Wolman grew up in rural Shenandoah, Pennsylvania. He often hitchhiked to Philadelphia and stood outside the gate at Shibe Park. The security guard usually waved him in by the third quarter. He was a dropout at J. W. Cooper High School and began driving a truck for his father, who was in the wholesale fruit and produce business. Not long after he married, Wolman and his wife, Anne, jumped into a 1938 Chevrolet coupe and headed blindly away from Shenandoah, just like they do in the movies. They had been living in a $6-a-week room, cooking meals on a hot plate. But they were too adventurous to stay away from the bright lights.

"Anne wanted to go to New York," Wolman said. "I liked Philadelphia. So we made a pact. We decided to pick up the first hitchhiker we saw and go where he was going." Near Mountain Top, Pennsylvania, they gave a ride to a George Washington University student. That's how Wolman's dream began.

The construction boom of the '60s was underway and Jerry Wolman rode it, earning enough money to outhustle three other groups for the Eagles on January 23, 1964, with a $5.5 million bid. He was only 36. Then came a terrible miscalculation. While Wolman was occupied with the Eagles, his company began work on a 103-story, $50 million office-apartment complex in Chicago known as the Hancock Center. The project became tangled in mistakes relating to the foundation. Wolman's company eventually went broke, and he lost everything, including his beloved Eagles.

"We had caisson failures," said Wolman. "They were big, round tubes that were put into the ground and then cement was poured into them. That's where it all went wrong. It was the way the caissons were pulled. When all was said and done, we probably lost $20 million."

Soon checks were bouncing from the club's bank account. At least two clubs, Cleveland and Pittsburgh, reported they were owed visiting team guarantees from the previous season. Wolman's boyhood dream eventually ended up in a Baltimore bankruptcy court. Wolman, who enjoyed spending money on others, was $72 million in debt.

Wolman, playing bad odds, couldn't pull it off. His reorganization plan stalled in the courts, like Joe Kuharich's offense. He eventually sold the club in 1969 to Leonard Tose, a colorful trucking executive, for $16.1 million. Six years later, a federal judge ruled that Wolman's buy-back arrangement with Tose was nullified by an August 1, 1969 deadline. Wolman was officially an ex-owner.

"First of all, it was a bit of an ego trip, which is the case with most owners," said Wolman. "I thought of the team becoming a winner. For me, it was a boyhood dream. The Eagles were my team. I still feel a great deal of loyalty to the Eagles. I love Philadelphia. I love the people of Philadelphia. And I love the fans. We had crabfests there. We invited the players' wives. We were all very close, more like a family."

If he had kept the Eagles, Jerry Wolman had planned to replace Joe Kuharich as head coach. So was Kuharich's 15-year contract a mistake? "Probably not," said Wolman, hedging his answer. "I liked Joe. Probably the game had passed him by a little bit. He was a God-fearing guy. But I probably would have moved him up in the organization and hired a new coach."

Wolman says he thought about Bart Starr, Don Shula, and Vince Lombardi as possible coaches. As Wolman's Hancock project began failing, there were rumors that Lombardi was trying to buy the Eagles. Wolman said

Lombardi called him to knock down the stories. A year later, in 1969, Lombardi was hired to coach the Washington Redskins. "He gave me the season tickets that I still have," said Wolman, now a Washingtonian.

However, Wolman has a new attraction in the game. His grandson, Brian, is an acrobatic wide receiver at Hofstra University. "Here at Churchill [Maryland] High School, he caught 78 passes and scored 21 touchdowns," Wolman said. "He's only 5-foot-9 and a sophomore at Hofstra. I love to watch him play."

Since he lost the Eagles and then his wife, Anne, to a heart attack in 1971, Wolman has emerged with a new business and a new wife. He bought a spring water company in Clarksville, Maryland, that has grown beyond his business dreams.

"I didn't get remarried until '85," says Jerry Wolman. "That was too long to wait."

NORMAN BRAMAN

He was tall and youthful and he could tell you nostalgic stories about carrying a water bucket out to Steve Van Buren and the other Eagle stars of the '40s. Norman Braman used to sneak into Shibe Park to watch the Eagles dominate the league with their relentless style of play. There were the dreams of youth, but never the dream of owning the Eagles as the son of an immigrant barber from Poland.

Yet about 50 years after those sparing years in South Philadelphia, Braman had made a fortune in the luxury car business. He bought the Eagles from bankrupt owner Leonard Tose in 1985 for $67.5 million. Nine years later, he would sell the franchise to Jeffrey Lurie, a 42-year-old movie-maker and member of a Boston publishing house family, for $185 million, turning a profit of $117.5 million. Yet Braman insists the reason he sold the team had nothing to do with his wealth.

In his nine-year run as owner, Braman almost always found himself defending his sports decisions in business terms. He sold BMWs, Cadillacs, and other luxury cars for a living. He lived in Miami Beach and spent summers in a villa on the coast of France. His critics, therefore, assumed that Braman was lured out of the football business by Lurie's huge offer.

"When I went through surgery in 1991 on my cervical spine, it was very heavy-duty surgery," said Braman. "I made up my mind as an objective to

Norman Braman, who snuck into Shibe Park to watch the Eagles in the '40s, found success in the luxury car business and bought the Eagles in 1985 for $67.5 million.

strive to relieve the stress and pressure in my life." That's when Braman decided to sell the franchise, one of the most stable in the league.

"Sports are all-consuming, 365 days a year, 24 hours a day," said Braman. "And especially not living in Philadelphia. That made me realize it was over. It took me two and a half years to do it. But I have no regrets. I have other interests that keep me very, very occupied."

During the years that Braman owned the Eagles and commuted to games from Miami, the team was highly successful: five 10-win seasons from 1988-92. Yet the Eagles never reached the NFC title game, losing three first-round games and one divisional playoff. Braman became a convenient target for talk-show critics and writers when All-Pro defensive end Reggie White jumped to Green Bay after a contract dispute in 1993. On the other hand, Braman surprised Pro Bowl quarterback Randall Cunningham with a $4 million contract before an early-season game. And between 1989-91, salaries reflected anything but the careful hand of a tight-fisted owner. Salaries for offensive starters went from $5.083 million to $7.720 million, a 32.2 percent jump, while salaries for the defensive starters went from $4.360 million to $7.742 million, a 77.5 percent jump. The team salary in that same period jumped from $9.443 to $15.462 million, a 63-percent increase. And there were those club junkets in the off-season when Braman hosted the front office workers in balmy Florida.

"It was an unforgettable experience," said Braman. "They were wonderful years that I'll never forget. I don't look back with any regrets. It was terrific."

LEX THOMPSON

The life and times of Alexis Thompson were the equivalent of a double-reverse, followed by a lateral and then a deep pass to the opposite sideline. Thompson, an heir to a $6 million fortune in steel stocks (Inland Steel Co.), bought the Pittsburgh Steelers in 1939 for $160,000. He was only 30. Then he and Art Rooney, who had purchased a major interest in the Eagles, swapped franchises.

Thompson, a Yale graduate, hired Greasy Neale off the Bulldogs staff to coach his new team. Neale, all fire and brimstone, coached the Eagles to their first world championship in 1948, and then Thompson sold the team for $300,000 to a Philadelphia syndicate that came to be known as the "100 Brothers." The team trained at Saranac Lake, New York, where Thompson converted an empty tuberculosis sanitarium into a permanent training facility known as the Eagles' Nest. In between workouts, the players enjoyed water skiing and boating and played tennis and golf.

Steve Van Buren and Alex Wojciechiwicz loved those late afternoons when they would jump into an outboard motorboat and whiz around the lake. There often were impromptu races with other boaters. In one of them, Wojie fell overboard when the motor suddenly turned sideways. Still with his pipe in his mouth, Wojie splashed about, but couldn't escape the wayward boat, which kept circling in his direction, once knocking his pipe into the water. Wojie eventually made it to shore, muttering something about "that devil doing his best to kill me."

Thompson's camp was probably the first permanent training site for an NFL team. "He was a fine guy," said tackle Al Wistert. "First of all, he did not interfere with the coaching staff and the team. He gave them full authority. That was not true with Jim Clark and the hundred owners. Jim Clark was a trucking executive and he apparently was raised the hard way, too. He felt he wanted to interfere and help run the team. So they became enemies, the coaches and the owners. That's why Greasy [Neale] got fired."

Although Thompson never played football as a Yalie, he became a world-class bobsledder, often turning up at the runs in Lake Placid and St. Moritz. He also was an Olympian in field hockey in 1936.

Sports feats aside, Thompson's domestic life involved three marriages and two divorces. He was found dead outside his Englewood, New Jersey, apartment in 1954. Thompson, who had moved in high society and glamour circles, was 44.

BERT BELL

He moved the bankrupt Frankford Yellowjackets from the suburbs to Philadelphia and gave them a new name, the Eagles. He refused to surrender to the rival All-America Football Conference and negotiated a historic merger on his terms. He sold the owners on a blackout policy for home games. He helped create the annual college draft.

As an owner and then league commissioner, Bert Bell accomplished all of these things. Bell was raised on Philadelphia's Main Line. His first name was actually de Benneville, suggesting wealth and high society. The Bell family owned plush hotels and plenty of choice real estate. Yet Bert Bell never lost his love for the game he played at the University of Pennsylvania. So he flung himself into the sport, as an owner, coach, and eventually, in 1946, commissioner of the National Football League. He was an amazing visionary, even recognizing the fledgling NFL Players Association, when the big issues were the number of practice socks and the amount of fines for being late to meetings.

Bell and co-owner Lud Wray paid $4,500 for the Yellowjackets, a dreadful team that had folded after a 1-6-1 record in 1931. To save money, Bell became the team's coach, general manager, ticket manager, and press agent. The Eagles languished in the Eastern Division cellar for five straight years and endured 10 straight losing seasons. It took a one-year wartime merger with Pittsburgh, forming the so-called Steagles, to produce a winning record. Then the Eagles began hitting with draft choices, the biggest of them Steve Van Buren in 1944, and winning, on the field if not at the gate.

In 1946, Bell was named to succeed Elmer Layden as commissioner. His first decision was to move the league office from Chicago to Bala Cynwyd, a Philadelphia suburb.

Bell's first challenge was coping with the talent-rich AAFC. The new league, throwing money around like frisbees, signed Ace Parker, Bruiser Kinard, Crazylegs Hirsch, Otto Graham, Dante Lavelli, Marion Motley, and Frankie Albert. Bell, however, called the AAFC "the other league" and refused to submit to outside pressure for cutting a deal. The AAFC soon became a league of haves (Cleveland Browns, San Francisco 49ers) and have-nots (Chicago Rockets, Los Angeles Dons). Bell and AAFC legal counsel Arthur Friedlund eventually hammered out a merger agreement on December 9, 1949. Bell dictated most of the terms, including the addition of the Browns, 49ers, and Baltimore Colts to the NFL. That same year, the Eagles won their second straight NFL championship.

Perhaps the strongest stance taken by Bell related to television, then in its infancy. Bell reasoned that it made no sense to televise home games when fans were paying to enter the home stadium. "Television creates interest, and this can benefit pro football," said Bell. "But it's only good as long as you can protect your home gate. You can't give fans a game for free on television and also expect them to pay to go to the ball park to see the same game."

Bell was on the edge of another war in 1959 when the ambitious American Football League was formed. Sadly, Bell never got to mount up and fight the ensuing war. He died of a heart attack on October 11, 1959, while watching the Steelers and Eagles play at Philadelphia's Franklin Field, where he played as a collegian.

JEFFREY LURIE

Jeffrey Lurie walks with a certain bounce. And in his ninth year as owner of the Eagles, there is a stronger bounce to his step, reflecting the mood of an man who is at the top of his game.

From his second-floor office at the two-year-old NovaCare Complex, Lurie can see cranes in the distance, working the site of a new $512 million, 66,000-seat stadium set to open in 2003. Below, during workouts on fields trimmed like putting greens, Lurie can see his talented players flex their muscles and perform their assignments. The opening of the training complex itself ended a long history of shabby workout facilities unworthy of a Saturday morning semipro league.

"When I bought the team [for a whopping $185 million], I was hoping within the first four or five years that we could get a new stadium and a new training complex," said Lurie. "The politics took a few extra years. If I had been told I would have to spend another few hundred million dollars for the stadium, I probably would have been too frightened to complete the deal."

Jeffrey Lurie is a thoughtful man, obsessed with social issues and values as well as professional sports. All around him, there are signs that the Eagles have arrived as a highly competitive team that he says was one play from facing New England in the 2002 Super Bowl. Lurie suggests that if the complex and stadium projects had been on the books when he arrived, he might have lured Mike Shanahan as his head coach.

"My top two choices as coach were Jimmy Johnson and Mike Shanahan," he said. "Jimmy had a weather issue in Philadelphia. But Mike Shanahan— if you had a clue, wouldn't you go back to Denver, or stay on the West Coast [with the 49ers], versus going to one of the worst facilities in the NFL, a dungy, basement place, with no new stadium in sight? No plans. No legislative approval. No nothing. We couldn't get the top people we wanted."

Lurie's first coaching hire was Ray Rhodes, a firebrand defensive coach. Rhodes produced two 10-6 playoff teams but never got past the first round of the playoffs. In Rhodes' fourth year, a season of bickering and finger-pointing and three wins, the team collapsed. "I think where it started to go wrong was that Ray was such an emotional guy that he had trouble planning more than a couple of weeks," says Lurie. "That was his strength. But it also was his Achilles heel. Today, you've got to really plan where you want to be, roster-wise, salary-cap wise, and in cap management. Ray was just not as good a manager as he was a motivator, and you need both today."

Rhodes, of course, was stuck with some quarterbacks who "couldn't hit a bull in the ass with a pea-shooter from five yards away," as former coach Bill Austin once said. The Eagles had a deal in their pocket to sign Green Bay scrambler Mark Brunell, but it was bungled by the front office. "Mark would have been a great addition," conceded Lurie. "But I think getting him would have just delayed the inevitable. In this league, if you don't manage and plan effectively, you can have Michael Jordan play for you and it wouldn't matter here."

Jeffrey Lurie, a bouncy, compact man, comes from a suburban Boston family that owned a movie-house chain and later got into publishing, forming a $3.5 billion conglomerate. Later, Lurie became a Hollywood movie producer whose films reflected his interest in social issues and values. Visitors are invariably attracted to the prominent photos of Dr. Martin Luther King, Jr., Mother Teresa, and Dr. Jonas Salk in the lobby of the complex. "I feel like everyone should walk in every day with a perspective on life and the values of caring about other people," Lurie said. "The commonality with Dr. King, Mother Teresa, and Dr. Salk was that they cared for less fortunate people. I want that value to be on exhibit throughout our organization at all times. It's powerful."

Nine years ago, Lurie skipped a press conference to announce the signing of safety Greg Jackson, the team's first free-agent acquisition. Instead, he appeared at a children's welfare home near Veterans Stadium to help dedicate a new playground. "That's my values," said Lurie. "I always want that."

Lurie credits his father, Morris, with teaching him about values and the place of sports in his life. "I was nine when he died," said Lurie. "He was 42. I feel like I live close to him every day cause he always said to me, 'Jeffrey, don't ever be a bully.' That was one of his lines. Another was to treat people the way you would want to be treated." Thus Lurie wants his team to be known for its class and compassion for others. "Treat it with pride, and don't think you're buying Filene's Basement," he said. "You're buying Nieman-Marcus, so to speak, so treat it like Nieman-Marcus."

Two years before Morris John Lurie died of cancer, he and his seven-year-old son, Jeffrey, watched the historic Giants-Colts overtime championship game on television. "I think that game turned me on to NFL football for life," Lurie said. "I was never so impressed with the tension and excitement of a championship game coming down to sudden-death overtime...wow!"

Lurie was also obsessed with baseball. He was a good-field, poor-hit shortstop until suffering a knee injury in prep school. "The Cincinnati Reds came to Boston," he recalled. "I don't know how many of us there were at the tryout; a few hundred maybe. Oh, boy, I was very young and they liked my speed. But I couldn't hit a curve ball, ha-ha-ha-ha. That was the end of my baseball career."

LEONARD TOSE

He was once the playboy of pro football. He was trim and tanned in the winter. He wore $2,000 form-cut suits to the office, and his graying hair was always groomed, giving Leonard Tose the look of a GQ man. Tose's lifestyle was very expensive and very fast and took him to $1,500-a-night villas in Acapulco, Beverly Hills, Miami Beach, and the gambling meccas of Atlantic City and Las Vegas, which cost him a lot more.

By his own calculation, Tose lost $25 million at the blackjack tables, mostly at the Sands and Resorts casinos in Atlantic City. "I'm a compulsive gambler, and I drink," he once said during lunch at Bookbinder's, the Philadelphia seafood restaurant. He was a Scotch man all the way (Dewar's and Perrier with a twist). "Nobody's a good player when they're drunk," Tose said. "But I wasn't a good player when I was sober. Don't misunderstand me, there were times when I'd win a lot of money in one night. A million dollars some nights. But I've also lost a million in one night."

The losses kept mounting. But he kept playing his crazy game, caught up in the excitement and the sight of the crowd pressed against the tables. "Oh, shit, my glass was never empty," said Tose, who sued the two casinos for allegedly plying him with liquor to continue the frenzy of the night. "In the trial, they said nobody ever saw me take a drink, those bastards." He lost his suit against the Sands and reached a modest settlement with Resorts, estimated at $25,000. "I didn't have any lawyers," said Tose. "It takes a lot of money to get good lawyers."

After 16 years as an NFL owner and countless trips to the sun and the bright lights of the casinos, Leonard Tose found himself broke. In the sad, lonely years that followed, he was supported by a small circle of loyal friends, including his old Eagles coach, Dick Vermeil. Tose lived in a junior suite at a downtown hotel in Philadelphia. His lavish lifestyle came to mind only when old cronies gathered to remember the generosity of the man who at the time was 87 and a pauper.

"I don't spend any money," said Tose. "It ain't easy, but what's the alternative? What am I going to do, shoot myself? It's hell to be 80 and broke. But [bleep,] I'm not going to quit."

Away from the gaming tables, Tose would play the role of the host with the most. He often took his coaches on vacations to Acapulco. He once took Julius Irving, the former basketball star, and his wife on a European trip, spending $200,000 to charter a yacht. The trips are memories now. Many of Tose's old friends, among them George Halas, Art Rooney, Jimmy Hoffa, Frank Sinatra, and former mayor Frank Rizzo, are gone, too. So are his tan Rolls Royce, his $150,000 Eagles-green helicopter, his mansion in suburban Villanova, his summer home in Longport, New Jersey, and, of course, his football team.

Tose was left with one special memory, the highly successful charity he launched in 1973 known as Eagles Fly for Leukemia. "You know the story," Tose said. "Fred Hill [a tight end] came into my office with tears in his eyes, saying his daughter had leukemia. In those days, nobody had heard of leukemia. So I said, 'Fred, anything the Eagles have, you've got.' We had a fashion show that raised $500. I gave them the difference between that and $7,500. Then we got hooked up with Dr. [Audrey] Evans, the top person in the field at Children's Hospital. She said she would like to furnish a floor. She said it would cost $80,000." Tose asked her how much the entire wing would cost, furnishings and all. "Two million dollars," Dr. Evans said. "You've got it," said Tose.

The leukemia charity is still going strong. There are 216 Ronald McDonald houses in 20 countries where parents of young leukemic patients can stay overnight. "That's his legacy; that's his Super Bowl," said former general manager Jim Murray.

Tose had married and divorced four times. He once bought a $292,000 diamond ring for Andrea, his second wife. Years later, she would smile as she left a divorce hearing and utter a line right out of a Hollywood movie. "See you in Acapulco, Len," she said.

Tose's third wife, Caroline, was a stewardess. Tose won her attention with a bawdy compliment as she worked the first-class section. "Lady," Tose told Caroline, "you have a beautiful ass."

The beautiful women and the Rolls Royces. The balmy nights in Acapulco. The parties in New Orleans. The autumn Sundays in the owner's box, scotch in hand. Tose didn't care to remember the glittering fun of it all.

Once the playboy of pro football, former Eagles owner Leonard Tose ended up broke and living in a Philadelphia hotel.

Instead, he regarded his gambling losses like some badge of honor. Old friends who had drifted away were dismissed as snakes in the tall grass.

Tose would rise early in his hotel suite, usually about 5 a.m. He would read at least four daily newspapers, including *USA Today*, the *Philadelphia Inquirer* and *Daily News* and the *New York Times*. He also read novels and liked to quote Thoreau. Paula, an interior designer from Gladwynne, Pennsylvania, who was at least 35 years younger than Tose, and John Fitch, Tose's former chauffeur, were among the closest friends in his dwindling circle.

Sometimes Leonard Tose got carried away with his power. According to one NFL owner, Al Davis was throwing his own power around at a league meeting. Tose reportedly told the owner that he could get rid of Davis. Did Tose mean a hit? "You know, he was in the trucking business," laughed Jim Murray. "Jimmy Hoffa and he were people who worked together. And he watches a lot of those old George Raft movies."

After all those years, Leonard Tose still saw life in terms of the score. "You know, everybody wants to be with a winner," he said. "There's nothing wrong with that. But when you're a [bleeping] loser, you're a bum."

Tose certainly didn't look like a bum when we met again at the Radisson Plaza Warwick Hotel in downtown Philadelphia in the summer of 2002. He wore a cream-colored summer jacket and a blue shirt, with a matching pocket handkerchief. His gray hair had been trimmed, an old Tose custom. His only display of jewelry was his gold Eagles ring from the 1981 Super Bowl.

"I get tired easily sometimes," said Tose. "I walk every day, right up in the hallways. Each way twice is one mile, so I do four, which is two miles. Sometimes I think I'm 97. I was born in 1915, so I guess I'm really 87. Paula says I ought to do some volunteer work. I got some calls from the city about needing help with kids. So I volunteered and they never called back."

Tose spent a week in a city hospital for tests after suffering an intestinal problem. "They drew blood for a week," he said. "They took all the blood out of me. I didn't hear from anybody for a whole week." Tose claimed that neither the league nor some of his old fellow owners would even return his phone calls.

As for the story that he once said he could take out Al Davis, Tose nodded. "I saved his life," said Tose. "They were going to take his team away, and I testified for him. Now he hates me. I did tell somebody I could put him away. I told him, too. I don't live in fear."

Tose said he had tried to get a job as a salesman. "I could sell, I could do that," he said. "But nobody will hire me." His lips tighten and curled upward, Tose's way of showing scorn. He often cursed. But he would not beg for money or any other kind of handout. Leonard Tose got to his feet.

"I'm going to get a drink," he said, moving slowly across the lobby towards the hotel bar.

A year later, on a bright Easter Sunday, mourners gathered at the Tiferet Bet Israel Synagogue in suburban Blue Bell, Pennsylvania, to celebrate the memory of this son of a Russian immigrant. Leonard Tose died five days earlier at age 88.

"He was the most unique, most complex, most unselfish giver I've ever been around," said Dick Vermeil. "He was an original piece of work." Vermeil cried shamelessly at the podium that day. "No mistake," he said, "he tested life to an extreme. But when all was said and done, the only person he ever hurt was himself."

"He was one of a kind, like some unforgettable character from the Damon Runyan era," said Jim Murray. There will never be another Leonard Tose among the clubby NFL owners, and their meetings will never be as much fun for the participants or for the beat writers.

6

OTHERS WHO SERVED

BILL BAKER

Bill Baker was an Eagles scout in the years when teams relied more on National and Blesto combine reports and less on their own talent evaluators. He played at Tennessee and Wyoming and once coached an unbeaten team at Chadron State in Nebraska, and he could size up prospects without a stopwatch or tape measure.

In 1977, Baker liked a running back named Wilbert Montgomery from Abilene Christian. Montgomery had scored 76 touchdowns in a dazzling career. But he also had sustained a serious thigh injury as a senior. Yet Baker persisted in his evaluation of Montgomery as a legitimate prospect, knowing that trainer Otho Davis had a reputation for bringing them back from the whirlpool.

The Eagles eventually drafted Montgomery as a sixth-rounder. He played like a Heisman Trophy winner. Baker kept finding long shots like that, helping the Eagles become highly competitive after 10 straight losing seasons. They hit on halfback Billy Campfield and center Mark Slater at Nos. 11 and 12 in 1978, linebacker Al Chesley (11) in 1979, safety Ray Ellis (12) in 1981, defensive tackle Harvey Armstrong (7) in 1982, linebacker Seth Joyner (8) and defensive end Clyde Simmons (9) in 1986, and cornerback

Izell Jenkins (11) in 1988. And then, after that 1988 draft, Bill Baker was fired.

"I'm a damn good scout; anybody will tell you that, Buddy [Ryan] will tell you that," said Baker in his farewell to Philadelphia. "There are more guys I scouted on this team than Carter has pills. Now all of a sudden I'm let go."

How could a terrific scout like Bill Baker be given a one-way ticket to Tucson, Arizona, his hometown? Baker conceded that he had swapped scouting reports before the 1988 draft, giving the Blesto list to another scout for his National list. The practice is common around the league. As *USA Today's* pro football editor, I was always able to obtain both lists with their confidential player ratings.

Indeed, Pittsburgh coach Chuck Noll once asked, "Why belong to a scouting combine when we can get the list for 50 cents?" Both scouting services then began coding their reports. Not only coding but giving some mediocre players phony blue-chip grades. The Blesto report that *USA Today* published in 1988 was coded and turned out to be the Eagles version.

Baker never gave me any scouting information. Nor did the grades come from another scout with whom Baker swapped reports. Yet the story added wings when *Boston Globe* columnist Will McDonough wrote a bogus column about "the most wanted spy in the National Football League." McDonough didn't identify Baker until the following week when he gave the beleaguered scout a forum to plead his case. By then, Baker had been fired after owner Norman Braman had threatened to give each scout a lie detector test. Ironically, five of the Eagles' 11 picks that year were from Baker's western region.

"People on that team know me," Baker said. "They know I always tell the truth. But not one of them has had the guts to stand up for me. I know they thought I was the guy who gave it to *USA Today*. But hell, I knew Blesto had coded the numbers. So why would I go and give it to Gordon Forbes when I knew that? Nobody was going to fight for Bill Baker. It's almost as if I was set up or something."

They took away Bill Baker's job. But they couldn't take away his honesty and reputation. They remain to this day.

OTHO DAVIS

They kept filing into the First Presbyterian Church in Moorestown, New Jersey, thinking only of Otho Davis, the man they had just lost. The mourners included former Eagles players, a retired NFL security officer, former head coach Dick Vermeil, former general manager Jim Murray, video director Mike Dougherty, local players agent Jim Solano, and a large group of writers and sportscasters.

Davis passed away on May 2, 2000. He had been the Eagles' Texas-born head trainer for 23 years before losing a difficult fight with liver and pancreatic cancer. During the 90-minute service, Davis was eulogized in terms that were special and far beyond his career as a trainer.

"Sometimes people say professional football is a very nonpersonal sport," said former linebacker Frank LeMaster. "Otho really cared. He was like a dad."

Former quarterback Ron Jaworski remembered his friend's training room. "It was unique to anything I had ever seen," Jaworski said. "It was somewhat of a museum, all those old leather helmets and those steel nose guards. You never felt comfortable in those training rooms. But his was a place where you felt a little bit at home."

Davis used to con rookies with promises of free trips to the Atlantic City casinos and free turkeys at Thanksgiving. The casino bus and the free birds, of course, never showed up. "He'd feed them a urine pill before their first night off," Jaworski recalled. "It turned their urine deep blue. The next day, their faces got a little pale."

"Otho was a healer," said sportscaster Don Tollefson at the trainer's services. "He was a healer of the soul and mind more than the body." Or, as LeMaster put it, "Otho kept it light, and everybody had fun."

Davis was buried in Elgin, Texas, his birthplace, not far from where the Colorado River slowly winds to the Gulf of Mexico. Fittingly, the mourners sang one of his favorite hymns, "Near the Cross." "In the cross, in the cross, be my glory ever," they sang, "till my raptured soul shall find rest beyond the river." No Eagle who came under his care will ever forget this very special man.

LEO CARLIN

There were always tickets on the minds of the Carlin family. Leo Carlin, the Eagles' 64-year-old ticket manager, grew up knowing all about the business. His father was a Pro Bowler in the world of theatre tickets. So Leo learned how tickets appeared almost like magic for a sold-out show if the mayor happened to call. Or the boss.

Actually, Carlin has worked the windows for four of them: Jerry Wolman (1964-69), Leonard Tose (1969-1984), Norman Braman (1985-1994), and Jeffrey Lurie, the current owner. They all had their own personalities and sense of how to run a ticket operation. Carlin, who joined the Eagles family full-time in 1964 when game tickets were $5.50, can't quite believe the scope and operation of the new marketing department under Lurie.

"The world of sports business has taken a giant step from what it was," said Carlin. "The advent of so much more marketing under this regime is amazing." Lurie's marketing blitz (the club lists 22 employees in its sales and marketing office) better be good. The Eagles will move into a new 66,000-seat stadium in 2003, and Carlin must do a little marketing himself to introduce fans to a new buzz term, the permanent seat license. Yet Leo Carlin will never forget the old Vet, that 31-year-old monument to hard turf and mostly hard times.

In 1970, Carlin had moved his ticket operation to Veterans Stadium after years of a bandbox operation at 30th Street. A week later, city managing director Fred Colett informed the Eagles that the facility wouldn't be ready in time. "We moved everything back," said Carlin. "What a mess." There was an even faster flip-flop in 1968. Student unrest in Mexico City forced the Eagles to move a preseason game back to Franklin Field. "It was 48 hours of nonstop work," said Carlin.

He jogs four times a week when he isn't sweating though a hard game of racquetball. Carlin is a tough Philadelphian all the way, with a degree from St. Joseph's and a stint in the Marine Corps.

JIM GALLAGHER

From Dick Absher to Mike Zordich, Jim Gallagher has seen them all. The great ones, the not-so-great ones, and the flops. Jimmy Gal, his popular nickname in the business, served the Eagles for 46 years. The scorecard: four owners; 17 head coaches and at least 21 different starting quarterbacks.

Gallagher bounced from one job to the next after high school. After graduating from the local Pierce Business College, he worked in the University of Pennsylvania athletic office for $35 per week. Then he moved to the Pennsylvania Railroad office, bumped up to $50. Seven months later, he was hired by the Eagles.

"I was a stenographer," said Gallagher. "I worked with [general manager] Vince McNally, helping him contact college players. I also sold tickets and got sandwiches for the big shots. There were three girls in the whole organization. I'd even jump in and run the switchboard for an hour and a half at lunchtime. I'd answer the phone, 'Philadelphia Eagles...plenty of tickets left.'"

Gallagher used to turn up at the owners' meetings which were held in Philadelphia, rubbing shoulders with owners George Marshall, Dan Reeves, Art Rooney, and Tony Morabito. Former Eagles owner Bert Bell was then the commissioner, running the league from an office in suburban Bala Cynwyd. Gallagher eventually moved into the personnel office and then into public relations when the game became a television bonanza.

In the war years of pro football, Gallagher was often dispatched to sign the low-rounders. In 1964, he flew to Nashville, Tennessee, to coax a huge Tennessee A&I back named Israel Lang into signing as the Eagles' 18th-round pick. Lang was a redshirt junior, but the teams laughed at the rules in those years, signing anybody with talent.

"How's he look?" said McNally over the phone. "He's got enormous legs," said Gallagher. "Okay, offer him $12,000 and a $2,000 bonus." Gallagher's offer was too low, according to John Merritt, Lang's coach. "Up it a little," said McNally, knowing that San Diego and Kansas City were on Lang's trail, too. Gallagher's $14,000-and-$4,000 bid, and the promise of a box of choice cigars for Merritt, closed the deal. The check was scrawl-marked. Gallagher replaced the lower figures with the higher ones.

It was a time when teams subscribed to *Street & Smith*, the sports magazine, and sometimes made picks from impressive statistics and action photos.

Izzy Lang, Gallagher's guy, made it with the Eagles as a reserve fullback. He hammered away at defenses in a spot role, gaining more recognition for his massive thighs than his runs. In 1969, he was traded to the Los Angeles Rams for receiver Harold Jackson, a steal for the Eagles. Lang rushed for one yard in one carry, the last of his career.

Jim Gallagher kept grinding out those press releases for 21 more years before becoming director of alumni affairs in 1990 and retiring in 1995.

Ah, *Street & Smith* yearbooks. Baby-sitting rookies. Working the club switchboard. Hustling black-and-white game films to the Harrisburg airport in a borrowed car. Those were the days.

BOW WOW

If you believed him, which wasn't always possible, Bow Wow led an extraordinary life. His real name was Wojtkiewicz S. Wojchiechowicz. Almost everybody called him Bow Wow, his nickname from the years he hung around the football office at UCLA. Bow Wow answered the phone, brought back coffee for the Bruins coaches and got to know a workaholic head coach named Dick Vermeil. When Vermeil was hired by the Eagles in 1976, he brought Bow Wow with him.

"During the season, he acts as a valet for me," Vermeil said. "When things get a little grim, he can make me smile."

In the off season, Bow Wow would return to the glittering world of Beverly Hills and Hollywood, turning up at celebrity parties and telling everybody he was a Polish prince who had been married to Sheila Graham, the gossip columnist. But when you tried to call the number on his business card, it never rang. It turns out that Bow Wow's number in Trancas Beach, north of Malibu, was one digit short, Hollywood 9-125. Most of his tales of adventurous nights on the Hollywood scene seemed almost too exciting and too dramatic. As Dick Vermeil said, Bow Wow was a valet who ran for, but really didn't hang with, the Hollywood crowd.

CARL PETERSON

The cover of the 2001 Kansas City media guide presents a montage of two old football friends who almost seem joined at the hip. Carl Peterson and Dick Vermeil first met in Los Angeles in 1974. Vermeil, hired to succeed Pepper Rodgers as head coach, retained Peterson as his receivers coach and confidante. They have been almost inseparable ever since.

"Dick was on the staff of the Los Angeles Rams," said Peterson. "They would come to UCLA every year during spring practice. Then they would take us out for cocktails and dinner. They did the same cross-town with Southern Cal. It was really a recruiting ploy."

Peterson remembers his first interview with Vermeil. "It was between midnight and 3 a.m.," he said. "He was still on the Rams staff, sort of juggling two balls at the same time. But he knew a lot about me before the interview."

What followed was an amazing odyssey. Vermeil hired Peterson for his UCLA staff. When Vermeil became head coach of the Eagles, Peterson went with him, eventually becoming director of player personnel. When Vermeil retired in 1982 because of burnout, Peterson remained in Philadelphia near his old friend to run the Stars, the city's United States Football League team. They split in 1989 when Peterson made a career jump to take control of the struggling Kansas City Chiefs. A dozen years later, they were together again, Peterson now the boss and Vermeil his head coach.

"I shudder to think where I would be without Dick Vermeil," said Peterson. "Dick gave me more responsibility and more authority in my career. I remember when Herman Ball retired from the personnel office. Dick called me in and asked if I wanted to move into personnel. I told him I'd really like to be the guy doing the hiring and firing." This little interchange followed:

Vermeil: "So, you want to be the guy who fires me."

Peterson: "No, you're the guy who hired me."

Vermeil: "But you could fire me."

Peterson: "No, I can't do that, because you hired me."

Carl Peterson laughed easily. Dick Vermeil was back in his football life, hired by his old friend. They started together on the West Coast, moved together to the East Coast, and then were reunited in the country's Heartland.

Peterson has grown very rich in Kansas City, improving the Chiefs with major moves and giving owner Lamar Hunt sellouts every Sunday. The Monday night games at Arrowhead Stadium have become celebrations, with Peterson inviting stars of the sports and entertainment world to be part of the fun. Peterson himself usually turns up on game days in a stylish trench coat, wearing dark glasses.

Yet of all the times in Peterson's life, none can rival those special years in Philadelphia. Especially when he pulled off the two best deals of his career: drafting halfback Wilbert Montgomery in 1977, the first year he headed the personnel office, and drafting receiver Mike Quick in 1982.

The Eagles had a cornerback named Joe (Bird) Lavender, who failed to report to training camp. Peterson, with Vermeil's blessing, shipped Lavender to George Allen in Washington, for tackle Manny Sistrunk and three draft picks. One of those, a sixth-rounder, was used to draft Montgomery, a darting runner from Abilene Christian, who would become a Pro Bowl back.

"Wilbert had scored 69 touchdowns in college," recalled Peterson. "I told Dick, 'That's hard to do against the Sisters of the Poor.' We brought him, in and he was scared to death. But he made our team despite a quad injury. In

Carl Peterson served Dick Vermeil's Eagles teams in a variety of roles.

the last regular-season game in '77 against the New York Giants, he started and gained 130 yards. Wilbert made us so much better."

Just before the 1982 draft, Vermeil called an old coaching buddy in Buffalo, Chuck Knox. They talked about prospects. Vermeil confided that the Eagles planned to draft Perry Tuttle, a highly productive receiver from Clemson. Knox, however, pulled off a trade with Denver the next day, jumping one spot ahead of the Eagles and picking...Perry Tuttle.

Peterson admonished Vermeil for "talking to old friends before the draft" and then returned to the draft board. "We had Mike Quick as the next receiver," said Peterson. "Dick kept coming up with different names. Quick hadn't caught many passes, but they had run the option at North Carolina State. [Receivers coach] Dick Coury pushed for him and we finally took him. Mike Quick went to five Pro Bowls."

Tuttle, on the other hand, caught only 25 passes in a brief three-year, three-team career plagued by injuries. This was a very lucky pick for the Eagles. So was Montgomery, who had flunked his predraft physical in New England because of a calcium deposit on his leg. Luck, as they say, is the residue of planning and plotting, or something like that. Say this for Carl Peterson, he always knew what he wanted, and he planned and plotted to achieve those goals.

Peterson still feels the Eagles were the best team in Super Bowl XV, a drab game lost to the Oakland Raiders. "We won 12 games that year and beat them earlier," said Peterson. "Then we won a couple of more in the playoffs. Against Dallas in the title game, that day, that year, that game, we were as high as you could get. Then we sank so low after losing the Super Bowl."

Now Peterson wants to get back to the big one. He hired Dick Vermeil to get him back. "If we make it," says Peterson, "Dick would be the only coach to take three different teams to the Super Bowl."

JIM MURRAY

The suspicion lingers that Jim Murray can always be found in his marketing office, at a church mass or funeral service, at some Philadelphia charity event, or at some nearby race track. Murray, who grew up in West Philadelphia, loves to move and shake within the city. And in the company of movers and shakers, he loves to tell stories, usually with some analogy about life or religion.

"I guess God took him because He didn't want him to see the end of the Raiders game," Murray will say, referring to the death of former Eagles coach Joe Kuharich on the morning of Super Bowl XV in 1981. Owner Leonard Tose took Murray out of the Villanova public relations office and kept promoting him, all the way to the general manager's office in 1974. Eventually, Murray became Tose's confidante and constant traveling companion. His world widened and glittered. Suddenly, there were trips with Tose to Acapulco, Beverly Hills, and Miami Beach, places in the sun with swaying palm trees and balmy breezes, and, as Murray once said, "empire-sized beds."

But now, Jim Murray should be bitter. He was fired as the Eagles' bubbly, story-telling general manager in 1983, just two years before Tose's fast lifestyle forced him to sell the team. Yet there are too many fond memories to throw mud on Tose's $2,000 suits with the morning-fresh creases. Besides, Tose was the one who helped start the Eagles Fly for Leukemia, Murray's favorite charity.

"I'll just say there was a big difference of opinion between Leonard's daughter and myself," said Murray, referring to Susan Fletcher, the hand-picked heir to the team and its vice president and legal counsel. "Susan and I have mended our ways. She now helps out at St. Christopher's Church. It was a tough part of Leonard's life. When we made up, I said that if I had stayed, he'd never have lost the Eagles. And I believe that. We had gotten out of much tougher jams than that."

Murray was a different kind of general manager. He would have felt out of place staying in some Holiday Inn in Boondocks, Mississippi, timing some draft prospect with a stopwatch. He was a city neighborhood guy who loved people, as well as charity events and fast horses. "You know what you're talking about?" Murray said rhetorically in the midst of discussing the Eagles' loss in Super Bowl XV. "The old neighborhoods. That's what the Eagles are. The Eagles are the quintessential old Philadelphia neighborhood, where everybody pitches in and helps each other. Pro football here may be a big business. But it's also probably something so special that it's hard to define."

Murray was regarded by Tose as a blood brother until their split. When Tose and the Eagles launched their highly successful charity for leukemia, Tose dug for the money. Murray did the legwork. And he's still running for the Ronald McDonald Houses, where parents of leukemic children can stay while treatment is given to their young offspring.

The date and the place are etched in Murray's mind. "October 15, 1974," he said. "4032 Spruce Street." That was the first Ronald McDonald House. "A little seven-bedroom home," said Murray. "Today, as we sit here on May 30, 2002, there are 216 houses in 20 countries. So it proves the power of sports for the good, a marriage of McDonald's and the Eagles."

Over the good years, Tose and Murray were almost always together on vacations and league-related trips. When Tose needed a table at Brennan's, the legendary New Orleans restaurant, Murray would peel off a dozen $100 bills to get his boss's party seated. When Tose interviewed Dick Vermeil for the vacant coaching job in 1976, Murray used the power of the buck to extend their stay at the Beverly Hills Hotel. When Tose underwent open-heart surgery in 1978, Murray rushed to a Houston hospital after the Miracle of the Meadowlands game in which the Eagles won on a bizarre fumble return.

"All [Giants quarterback] Joe Pisarcik had to do was genuflect," said Murray. "Of course, we signed Joe a couple of years later. I said, 'Let's give him some extra money just for not genuflecting.'" Jim Murray laughed at the memory, his Irish face alive with mirth. Murray, who made a remarkable jump from public relations staffer in 1969 to general manager at age 36 in 1974, defines his pro football experience by two events: the NFC championship win over Dallas in 1980, and the ongoing Ronald McDonald project.

"It was the coldest day of the year when we played the Cowboys," recalled Murray. "I never took myself seriously. But I took my job as a sacred trust. What the Eagles meant to the city, that gift was given back that day. Every real Eagles fan remembers every play of that game. You hate to say the Super Bowl was anticlimactic, but it really was a letdown."

Murray still works the city streets and corporate offices for McDonald's and is in constant touch with Kim Hill, the daughter of an Eagles player who inspired the leukemia drive. "September 11 gave us a line about unsung heroes," he said. "The people taking care of those McDonald's houses, the house managers, they're like unsung heroes, too."

MIKE DOUGHERTY

It was late in the 1978 season, or maybe 1979. Mike Dougherty, the video director, can't quite remember the exact season. Whatever the year, it was a fuzzy day. "It was at JFK Stadium in late November," he said. "The lightning came out of nowhere and hit the metal camera. I had my face up against the lens of the camera and could feel it hit. What little hair I have stood straight up."

Dougherty, a 27-year veteran of shooting game and practice tapes, was on the team's 40-foot lift. "I looked down and saw all the players [diving] on the ground," he said. "I got zapped, and I was shaking so badly that [assistant coach] Fred Bruney had to take the lift down."

Dougherty got the video job when Dick Vermeil arrived as head coach in 1976. He had been assisting Lou Tucker, who ran Tucker Sports Films, a private business. Vermeil wanted a full-time film guy, so Dougherty was hired as a full-timer. "In the off-season, I'd put together book binders and put the [draft] names on the board. I'd pick up guys at the airport, take them to physicals and then out to dinner and back to the airport. The young guys now don't understand how much we did back in those years."

Every April, Dougherty works the draft phone in New York. The Eagles make their picks in their war room in Philadelphia and phone their choices to Dougherty, who scribbles the names on cards to make it official.

"I think Mike Quick [1982] was the first guy," said Dougherty. "But Jon Harris [1997], Mike Mamula [1995], Antone Davis [1991], and Leonard Renfro [1993], who the hell were these people?" Harris and Renfro lasted two years with the Eagles. Mamula hung around for six years, Davis for five, but both were average players.

Dougherty's most memorable draft came in 1999. A busload of Eagles fans acted like the Ricky Williams fan club, screaming for their team to take the wonder back with the second pick. Instead of Williams, however, the Eagles selected Donovan McNabb, an option quarterback from Syracuse. The choice was greeted by jeers that bounced off the ceiling of the Theatre at Madison Square Garden and cut all the way to the stage.

"It was embarrassing," recalled Dougherty. "I'm just glad we were on the other side of the audience. Those clowns might have started throwing things, and it could have gotten ugly." Of course, McNabb emerged as a young superstar. Williams, drafted by New Orleans, was traded to the Miami Dolphins. Presumably, his old Philadelphia fan club has dispersed.

DR. JAMES NIXON

He wore bow ties and had a droll sense of humor. Somehow, Dr. James Nixon was also able to cope with the demands of the media on one hand and the silence of the head coach on the other. He graduated from the University of Pennsylvania Medical School in 1949, the same year the Eagles won their second NFL championship. From 1962-70, he was the team physician and chief orthopedic surgeon. He called himself simply "Doc," and one year he distributed a so-called "missive" to reporters, complete with diagrams of the skull and the knee, ankle and shoulder joints.

"Good chroniclers of the passing scene," wrote Dr. Nixon, "lay aside your quills and Remingtons and attend me, for I've got some facts and thoughts and things in defense of this fair physic.

"Opposable thumb aside, man is not as other living things, because he speaks. Speaking, he advances when there is agreement between men as to what is said. For with agreement, he is able to measure, and with measurement, is able to describe with accuracy. For little can be known unless it can be described or measured with accuracy. The greater the precisions of measurement, the greater the depth of knowledge.

"So, great, baby, give me the facts, but don't snow me. Tell it like it is, and why, and for how long. Lay it on me, man. We've got to communicate—the language gap—and thus the purpose of this missive."

Using Dr. Nixon's 32-page booklet, we were able to differentiate between a sprain and a strain and learn that the skull is composed of eight bones. Describing the complexity of the knee joint, he quipped: "While mother nature might have come up with a better design through evolution, this would have required an early form of football played by our tadpole ancestors." He was one helluva doctor.

7

VICK'S BAG OF TRICKS HAS EAGLES FEELING SUPER (AGAIN)

MICHAEL VICK IN THE SUPER BOWL

n Vick's years as an exciting but scattershot quarterback with the Atlanta Falcons, that idea seemed improbable. For all of the highlight tapes Vick filled, he was barely a 50 percent passer who never really learned how to manage the game. Later, of course, when Vick was incarcerated for his role in a violent dog ring operation, the idea of a Super Bowl was impossible.

But now there is legitimacy to the thought that Vick, hardly your classic pro quarterback with a six-foot frame and unpredictable moves, could lead his new team, the Philadelphia Eagles, to their first Super Bowl title. In Philadelphia, where talk of a Super Bowl is always in the air, Vick's magical 2010 season only encouraged the talkers.

"That's what I shoot for every year, the Super Bowl," said Andy Reid, the Eagles thoughtful head coach. "There's no more pressure than in the past. There's no more pressure they can put on us than I put on myself. It's always our No. 1 goal."

Reid has surrounded Vick with an impressive cast. There is blazing receiver and halfback speed, more than the Eagles have ever had. There is a collection of solid drive-blockers, all in their prime years. There is a reshaped linebacking corps that can fly to the ball. The blitzing, risk-taking defense had 39 sacks last year. The Eagles should have more this season with the continued presence of Pro Bowler Trent Cole and the return of former No. 1 draft pick Brandon Graham from knee surgery. Both are impressive sack makers from the flanks. And in the close ones, the Eagles can trot out Mr. Sure Foot, kicker David Akers, the only player left from Reid's team that lost a ping-pong Super Bowl after the 2004 season.

Reid's only possible concern is his veteran secondary. That unit always had a hard edge to it, nasty and relentless. But safety Brian Dawkins seemed to take that back-alley reputation with him when he departed two years ago for Denver. The Eagles gave up 31 touchdown passes last year and didn't intimidate anybody like Dawkins or the other departed bangers used to do.

Yet, even with modest improvement on the defensive side, the Eagles are definitely a Super Bowl threat, simply because of what Vick can do with a football in his hands. Despite missing four games (three with a rib injury), Vick passed for 3,018 yards and 21 touchdowns and scrambled for 676 yards and nine more touchdowns. He threw only six interceptions and finished with a stunning quarterback rating of 100.2. Accordingly, Vick was voted the league's Comeback Player of the Year, a crazy enough honor considering that he opened the season as a wide receiver in Reid's Wildcat scheme. That was his customary role in 2009.

And after the 10-6 season ended with a first-round playoff loss to Green Bay, Reid was pressed to explain Vick's remarkable turnaround. "He came out of prison with just a super attitude," said Reid. "He's been like a sponge with things and taken everything in. And it became neat to see the progress he's made and see him attack this issue."

Donovan McNabb, Vick's predecessor, took the Eagles to the Super Bowl in 2004 with the best season of his 11-year career in Philadelphia. McNabb passed for 3,875 yards and 31 touchdowns and was rewarded with a quarterback rating of 104.7, a club record. Yet, after the Super Bowl loss to New England, there was bickering in the ranks, most of it coming from malcontent receiver Terrell Owens. Reid kept coaching them with his fine hand, but the Eagles kept circling the Super Bowl, looking for a parking spot.

Knowing that McNabb would age and could face more injuries, Reid couldn't resist the opportunity to add a young successor. It came at the top of the 2007 draft. Reid snapped up Kevin Kolb, a kid from deep in the heart of Texas. Kolb didn't have McNabb's arm strength, but he was not only younger (23) than McNabb (then 31) but more nimble, with a quicker release. Three years later, Reid followed the old rule about getting rid of your fading talent before their skills deteriorate. The shocker was that Reid broke another old personnel rule: Never trade your quarterback within the division. Nevertheless, McNabb was dealt to the rival Washington Redskins for two draft picks. Then Reid made the call to Kolb in Granbury, Texas with the good news.

"He said, 'Hey, look, I'm going to make you the starting quarterback of the Philadelphia Eagles,'" recalled Kolb. "Obviously, I was fired up. Then he told me he had traded Donovan to Washington. I had been dreaming about this my whole life. You know, there's only 32 of you in the whole world. So it's pretty special."

Over the highly competitive years, Andy Reid has developed a reputation as a risk taker. Yet, he insists there wasn't any risk involved in the McNabb trade. "As long as the compensation was right (No.2 and No. 4 draft picks), I didn't consider it a risk," Reid said. "And I wanted it to be a good deal for him, too, And, in fact, it was."

With McNabb gone, Kolb became the new starter in Philadelphia. Behind him was Vick, who had been signed in the summer of 2009 as a spot player, primarily for Reid's offbeat Wildcat set. In the Wildcat, quarterbacks, receivers and running backs flip-flop positions to confuse a defense. But then Kolb suffered an opening-day concussion when he was whacked by Green Bay linebacker Clay Matthews. Michael Vick became the big man in Reid's rhythmic West Coast offense that day, and for the rest of the season. Vick quickly seized the moment. After all those nights of tape-watching and days of mastering Reid's playbook, he was now mentally into the game; sharp and quick with his decisions. And on one unforgettable Monday night in Landover, Maryland, while the Redskin fans, as well as some his Philadelphia critics, gaped in disbelief, Vick played a game that was not only thrilling but near perfect.

Vick led the Eagles to touchdowns on their first five possessions. After less than 16 minutes, the Eagles were romping, 35-0. Vick kept running those Reid bootlegs and scrambling along improvised running lanes that the Redskins always seemed to close too late. At the end, when Vick had finally stopped throwing and weaving his magic, he had produced an epic 59-28 win for Reid and his Eagles. Several days later, the Pro Football Hall of Fame called to obtain Vick's jersey.

"When he was in Atlanta, he'd look for one guy, and if he didn't come open, he was looking to escape the pocket," said former Eagles quarterback and ESPN analyst Ron Jaworski. "Now he is more inclined to stay in the pocket, go through his progressions and find No. 2 and No. 3. Michael has taken ownership of this offense. He wasn't interested in doing that when he played with the Falcons."

Of course, there was more to the story of Vick's breakout year than just his grim determination; his focus on reads and and post-practice study habits. Around Vick, Andy Reid placed some of the best offensive tools he has ever had.

THE KEY GAME-BREAKERS

Wide Receiver Jeremy Maclin: Caught 70 passes and scored 10 times in 2010, flashing his sprinter's speed and nasty attitude. "When he's out there, he's an animal," says Brent Celek the tight end. "When we're going to run the ball, he's out there chopping people downfield. He's angry, He's angry all the time." Maclin was just 21 when the Eagles drafted him at the top of the 2009 draft.

Wide Receiver/Kick Returner DeSean Jackson: Probably the fastest and certainly the most explosive player in the league. In three seasons, Jackson produced these amazing stats: 171 catches; 3,124 yards; 18.3 yards per-catch; 17 touchdowns, plus four punt return touchdowns. His 65-yard punt return last season as time expired capped a miracle 38-31 win over the New York Giants. The Giants led, 31-10, with only 8:17 left to play. But Vick inspired the comeback and Jackson delivered the knockout punch, taunting the Giants as he tip-toed into the end zone.

Tight End Brent Celek: Taken as an afterthought (lower fifth-rounder) in the 2007 draft that also produced Kolb and cerebral middle linebacker Stewart Bradley, Celek outplayed his rating. Wedging his way into the starting lineup in 2009, Celek played on the wild side, finding the seams for 76 catches and giving defenders the forearm, the high knee kick and everything else he could think of. And soon the PR office was cranking out those gee-whiz releases about Celek (24); Maclin (21) and Jackson (23) being the first NFL trio of 24 years old and under to have 50 or more catches and 750 or more yards. "When I have the ball, I try to be like Jerome Bettis," said Celek. "The first guy never took him down. He was a beast."

Halfback LeSean McCoy: Brian Westbrook was gone. So was Correll Buckhalter. But Andy Reid could never find that elusive back with a wiggle and a burst until McCoy popped up in the middle of the second round of the 2009 draft. The next season, as Westbrook's replacement, McCoy rushed for 1,080 yards. Not only that, he caught 78 passes, a lot of them check-offs from Vick. "He was more deliberate and accurate with his cuts," said Reid. "He's seeing daylight and getting north and south, which you have to do in this league. So, he learned, got stronger and it paid off for him."

Assuming the same starters return, the Eagles' big-play offensive unit will average 26.6 years, two years younger than Reid's Super Bowl team (28.5). Vick (31) will be the only starter in his thirties.

Reid's defense is older, with speed rusher Juqua Parker; corner Asante Samuel and strong safety Quintin Mikell all in their 30s. The Eagles will again function as one of the league's most notorious blitzing units. They storm and penetrate on almost any down, from almost every angle. The free-wheeling defense reflects Reid's personality as a confident risk-taker.

The difference on defense this year is the boss, not the scheme. Juan Castillo, the offensive line coach whose first love has always been defense, became Reid's new defensive coordinator. Castillo was part of a 1-2 shift. First, Reid lured Howard Mudd out of retirement from a Leisure World community in Mesa, Arizona. Then he replaced his young defensive coordinator, Sean McDermott, with Castillo. Reid gave it the old "different direction" line when explaining the move. Yet, there were also some cold numbers that ran through Reid's mind: the 35-32 squeaker win over Detroit; the 37-19 loss to Tennessee and the 31-26 loss to Chicago. The Lions, Titans and Bears ranked 17th, 27th and 30th in offense last year. Overall, Reid's defense gave up 43 touchdowns, five more than the previous year under the late, great Jim Johnson.

"I love these challenges," said Reid after elevating Castillo and handing the 69-year-old Mudd a coaching whistle. "This game is a game of risks. Everywhere from third-and-two to however you put this thing together, it's a game of risk. So I don't worry about that at all." As for Mudd, Reid came right out with it, calling his new man "a Hall of Fame caliber" offensive line coach. "To get him to come back was an important piece of the puzzle," Reid noted. "I can't wait to get everybody here and get this thing rolling. It's exciting."

Castillo will coach virtually the same unit that allowed 377 points, the most of any Andy Reid-coached team except for his injury-riddled 2005 defense (388). "We are going to be fast, physical, and fundamentally sound and be the best defense in the NFL," predicted Castillo. "We have good players here." Said Reid: "He's a phenomenal teacher.

THE KEY DEFENDERS

Defensive end Trent Cole: A relentless pass-rusher, Cole personifies the kind of player that Reid loves to coach. In the past three seasons, two of them Pro Bowl seasons, Cole totaled 31½ sacks, often rushing against extra blockers. "I don't care what it takes, I'm going to get there," insisted Cole, the son of a pastor and the 146th player (fifth round) taken in the 2005 draft that also produced two other starters: defensive tackle Mike Patterson and guard Todd Herremans.

Middle backer Stewart Bradley: One of Reid's football-smart, read-and-react defenders, Bradley was never far from the ball. The concern with Bradley: injuries. He missed the entire 2009 season with a torn knee ligament and the last four games in 2010 with a dislocated elbow. Jamar Chaney, his young backup, is built along the lines of old-school middle backers (6-0, 242) and is a promising run-stopper but doesn't have Stewart's range or size.

Cornerback Asante Samuel: A playmaker in defending against the pass, the former New England superstar had seven interceptions last year (in 11 games), two against Peyton Manning and two against brother Eli Manning. In his eight-year career (including postseason), he's picked off 49 passes, eight of which he took to the house, as they say, for touchdowns. The knock on Samuel is his inability to wrap up ball carriers. But how many NFL corners are great tacklers? They're backpeddlers and hip-movers, drafted for their ballhawking, and that's what Samuels does so well.

So the Eagles have youth, speed and playmakers up and down their units. And, most importantly, they have a new, dedicated quarterback who draws inspiration from his failed career in Atlanta. Vick now says he used "65 percent" of his ability in those early years when he would drop back, read his primary receiver, then take off if there was a defender lurking nearby.

Brian Billick, the former Baltimore Ravens coach, knows all about the quarterbacks who make it and the ones who flop. "It's a matter of if it all comes together mentally," said Billick. "Can they adapt themselves to what is an incredibly fast-paced and decision-laden position? You really need a guy who understands defenses." Says Miami offensive coordinator Dan Henning: "Give me a quarterback who can use the clock and work the chains."

Vick now understands what Billick and Henning meant. He entered his ninth, and most anticipated, season with playmakers everywhere: remarkable team speed, decent pass protectors, and drive blockers. Jackson, Maclin, Celek and underrated slot guy Jason Avant as receivers; McCoy as a slash-and-draw runner when the defense overplays for the pass.

Yet, Vick's big edge will be on the sidelines, the big man wearing a headset and plotting his next move, perhaps his next risk. Head Coach Andy Reid developed a feel for Vick's skills as Vick was developing a feel for Reid's offense. It was Marino and Shula in their early years. Montana and Walsh. Aikman and Johnson. Fouts and Coryell. Not the big numbers, of course, but the bond. Reid prefers to come out throwing, mostly from a shotgun formation, which is Vick's kind of scheme. Ideally, Reid likes a 60-40 pass-run mix. Vick, it turned out, was a perfect fit for what Reid and the Eagles wanted to do.

McNabb fitted, too. But Reid felt a change was needed after 11 seasons that produced six division titles and one NFC championship (2004) but no gleaming Super Bowl rings. Presumably, Reid feels an obligation to the city and its emotional fans to do more than just trot out Michael Vick and excite them.

"I love Philadelphia," the coach says. "The fans here are unbelievable. They're fair. If we stink, they let us know we stink. If we're doing okay, they let us know we're doing okay. But they're always there."

Reid has given them nine winning seasons and 128 wins. More than Mike Ditka gave Chicago and New Orleans. More than George Allen gave Los Angeles and Washington. More than John Madden gave Oakland. So, will Andy Reid finally hoist the Lombardi Super Bowl trophy over his head next February in Indianapolis?

Maybe, maybe not. Nothing is certain in pro football, a crazy game of variables, heartbreak finishes and debatable calls, made on the field and into the quarterback's radio helmet. Just ask Donovan McNabb, Reid's former star. McNabb ended the 2010 season on the Redskins' bench, a brooding man now uncertain of his future. Vick probably felt the same way until his career was rescued by Andy Reid, the big man on the sideline.

So, can Michael Vick emerge as the winning quarterback in the next Super Bowl? In the past 12 Super Bowls, none of the Comeback winners, among them Drew Brees (2004) and Tom Brady (2009), even made it to the Super Bowl after their special season. But at least Vick has a chance, something he didn't have when he was behind bars.

Vick, it must be noted, had the support of Eagles owner Jeffrey Lurie, as well as the head coach. "I feel like everyone should walk in (to the complex) every day with a perspective on life and the values of caring for other people," said Lurie, who has always been active in social issues. Indeed, there are huge photos of such noted social activists as Dr. Jonas Salk, Mother Teresa and Dr. Martin Luther King, Jr., in the lobby of the team's complex.

There was initial fear that animal rights groups would rally in protest at Vick's first home game on September 13, 2009. Yet, there was only a modest turnout, led by a small group of peaceful demonstrators. It was almost as if they had listened to Jeffrey Lurie and followed the word of Dr. King.

8

25 THINGS YOU PROBABLY DIDN'T KNOW ABOUT THE EAGLES

1. There were 20 veterans who crossed the picket lines in the 1974 players strike, including quarterback Roman Gabriel and linebacker Bill Bergey. The other strikebreakers: Jim Maxwell, Al Coleman, Tom McNeill, Johnny Outlaw, Roger Williams, Willie Germany, Bill Dunstan, Roy Kirksey, Jerry Patton, Don Zimmerman, Stan Davis, Bobby Picard, Kent Kramer, Steve Zabel, Frank Bosch, John Reaves, Kevin Reilly, and John Sodaski. Reaves, Reilly and Sodaski came to camp the day the strike ended.

2. Owner Lex Thompson once taught Steve Van Buren and Alex Wojciechowicz how to water-ski on Saranac Lake during training camp.

3. Pete Retzlaff was a world-class discus thrower in 1956 but was denied a chance to compete in the Olympics by AAU executive secretary Dan Ferris. Retzlaff, then in the service, had yet to sign an NFL contract but was prevented from becoming an Olympian because of his intent to play pro football.

4. Jon Brooks, a guard drafted as a second-rounder in 1967, once said he dropped the "h" in his first name so he could be quicker. Quick enough, it turned out, to be cut in his rookie year.

5. Halfback Ronnie Bull, a Chicago Bear who ended his career with the Eagles in 1971, claimed he could run blindfolded and tell which way the AstroTurf blades were slanted at the Vet.

6. Fullback Leroy Harris wore two different brands of shoes, one on each foot, in Super Bowl XV.

7. Coach Mike McCormack, seeking any kind of talent, held a free-agent tryout camp in 1973. A total of 406 prospects turned up at the old JFK Stadium and were timed, tested and then given free box lunches and "diplomas." One of the free agents was a female Long Island secretary who wore purple eye shadow and a smile for the coaches.

8. Linebacker Fred Whittingham, before starting his first game against the Cleveland Browns because of injuries, was asked how it felt to be playing against Leroy Kelly. Whittingham replied: "Who's Leroy Kelly?"

9. Thurman Randle, a 6-foot-6 rookie offensive tackle from Texas-El Paso, couldn't get out of bed after his first day in training camp in 1968. He was quickly cut but took his $6,000 bonus with him.

10. The Eagles once practiced at Murphy Field, an area owned by the University of Pennsylvania. The workouts were often punctuated by the screeching of brakes from motorists who could easily view the practices from a ramp off the Schuylkill Expressway.

11. Dave Graham, an offensive tackle, suffered an ankle injury just before the 1967 season opener. He was placed on injured reserve, meaning he was done for the year. But nobody told Graham, who was ready to play midway through the season. Once Graham and a trainer headed out to practice but found an empty field. Unknown to them, Coach Joe Kuharich had shifted the practice site to fool any potential spies from Washington.

12. Quarterback Norm Snead played with a tricky knee, so tricky that it would roll out if he happened to hook his toe on a bed sheet at night.

13. Owner Jerry Wolman, overjoyed to go to any playoff, paid for every check signed at a Bal Harbour, Florida, hotel during the 1966 Playoff Bowl (matching the conference runners-up). A lot of freeloading friends of friends turned up at the bar and restaurant each night.

14. John Carlos, the Olympic sprinter, was a 15th-round draft pick in 1970 but tore up his knee without being touched during an off-season workout. The Eagles tried to develop him into a kickoff returner, but it never worked out because of his poor hands.

15. Dave Lloyd, the starting middle line backer in the mid-'60s, never lifted weights, preferring to boast about his "natural strength."

16. Bill Dunstan, a journeyman defensive tackle in the early '70s, was called the toughest player he ever coached by assistant Jerry Wampfler.

17. Rich Kotite, the offensive coordinator under Buddy Ryan in 1990, was asked by owner Norman Braman which coach he most admired. "Don Shula," said Kotite, referring to the former Miami coach who was a close friend of Braman. The answer clinched the head coaching job for Kotite.

18. Harry Jones, the No. 1 draft pick in 1967, was shocked to learn he had been cut while reading the *Philadelphia Inquirer* at breakfast during the 1972 training camp. The Eagles, who didn't release the cuts until the day after notifying the NFL office, made it public later that morning.

19. At 5-foot-9, receiver Tommy McDonald is the shortest player ever selected to the Pro Football Hall of Fame.

20. Now in his 80s, All-Pro tackle Al Wistert starts each day with a workout that includes 17 different exercises (10 standing, seven prone). He finishes his regimen by peddling three miles on his exercycle.

21. Dick Vermeil held a training camp session on July 4, 1976, while the city was celebrating the bicentennial.

22. When coach Greasy Neale felt the Eagles needed inspiration, he turned the team over to All-Pro tackle Al Wistert for a Saturday pep talk.

23. Owner Leonard Tose once threw the greatest party of all on a 1971 preseason trip to Oakland. Every sportswriter from big and small papers was invited to a whirlwind weekend that included dinner at Ondine's, a fashionable restaurant in Sausalito, followed by a visit to the North Beach strip clubs in San Francisco.

24. Tim Rossovich, the free-spirited linebacker of the '70s, loved to see it rain during training camp at Albright. Rosso could then grab an inflated blocking dummy and ride the gutter water to the dressing room.

25. Buddy Ryan often changed quarterbacks, sometimes using Ron Jaworski on the first two downs and Randall Cunningham on third down. Yet there were never any bad feelings. Jaworski said they usually high-fived as they passed each other, "just like tag-team wrestlers."

ACKNOWLEDGMENTS

Pro football is a survivor's game, punishing and often violent. It makes demands on the human body that are almost cruel. Training camps, those six-week versions of a marine boot camp, start in the blistering heat of summer. Five months later, the season can end in frigid Buffalo, or Green Bay, where the hands, and sometimes the minds, are chilled to the bone. Injuries are common and "playing in pain" is an acknowledged concession to the game.

I would like to thank Joe Bannon, Jr., vice president and senior editor of Sports Publishing L.L.C., who suggested a book of tales about the Philadelphia Eagles. Derek Boyko and Rich Burg of the Eagles' public relations office were extremely helpful, as was aide Brian Cunningham, who patiently pulled out all the right files from a deserted information office at Veterans Stadium. Saleem Choudhry, a researcher at the Pro Football Hall of Fame, supplied me with the backgrounds on a number of Eagles greats, as did Larry Weisman, my *USA Today* colleague. Karen Schebesta-Donohue, a computer wizard, gets credit for formatting the stories and guiding me through the jungle of the Internet.

There are too many coaches to mention. But I would be remiss if I didn't cite Edgar Bright, my old head coach at Patchogue (N.Y.) High School, who took a chance on a 14-year-old sophomore quarterback when his starter went down. There were also a number of high school coaches in Jacksonville, Florida, including Tuffy Thompson, Bobby Varn, Don Jarrett, Pete Vas, and Virgil Dingman. They provided invaluable insight into this crazy, wonderful game during those chat sessions long ago.

Finally, I want to thank my partner, Marie Schebesta, who accepted the nights of writing *Tales from the Eagles Sidelines*. The long hours might have been painful, but she, too, lived up to the unwritten code of the game.